D1035041

387
51

Sacco-Vanzetti

HOWE LIBRARY
SHENANDOAH COLLEGE &
CONSERVATORY OF MUSIC
WINCHESTER, VA.

Sacco-Vanzetti:
Developments and Reconsiderations–1979

Conference Proceedings

BOWIE LIBRARY
SHENANDOAH COLLEGE &
CONSERVATORY OF MUSIC
WINCHESTER, VA

Boston, Trustees of the Public Library of the City of Boston · 1982

Copyright © 1982 by the Trustees of the Public Library of the
City of Boston

Library of Congress Cataloging in Publication Data:

Main entry under title:

Sacco-Vanzetti, developments and reconsiderations, 1979.

    Papers presented at a conference sponsored by and held at
the Boston Public Library, October 26–27, 1979.
    1. Sacco-Vanzetti case—Congresses. 2. Trials (Murder)—
Massachusetts—Dedham—Congresses. 3. Felicani, Aldino, 1891–1967—
Congresses. I. Boston Public Library.

KF224.S2S24	345.73'02523	81-12986
ISBN 0-89073-067-9	347.3052523	AACR2

Designed by Richard Zonghi

KF
224
.S2
S24
1982
343.52 Sa14s

Sacco-Vanzetti,
  developments and
  reconsiderations, 1979

All illustrations are reproduced from materials in the
Felicani Collection of the Sacco-Vanzetti papers
unless otherwise indicated.

Frontispiece: Aldino Felicani shortly after his arrival in
America, *circa* 1915.

Contents

HOWE LIBRARY
SHENANDOAH COLLEGE &
CONSERVATORY OF MUSIC
WINCHESTER, VA.

Goldberg

18.00

9.8.86

Dedicated to

ALDINO FELICANI, whose commitment to a case and a cause preserved a significant piece of history in the Felicani Archives, and to

FRANCIS MOLONEY, whose insight and energy made this conference on Sacco and Vanzetti a reality

Preface

Assembled here are the papers and statements delivered at the conference on Nicola Sacco and Bartolomeo Vanzetti, sponsored in October, 1979, by the Boston Public Library. The presentations included in this volume have been modified for publication in varying degrees, according to speakers' styles of delivery. Some speakers "read" prepared papers and, hence, altered them minimally for publication; others prepared their material "to talk" and, resultantly, revised their work for the change from oral form to print. Is it important to note, however, that the total substance of the two-day conference is recorded in its original form of delivery in the sound archives of the Library.

Professor Salomone has very effectively described the process and rationale of putting messages delivered from the podium into published form: "In speaking we do not realize how many unwanted hesitations, wrong starts, superfluities, wrong words, etc. we speak." As he suggests, because of these patterns of delivery, speakers may choose to take the "liberty of 'streamlining' some phrases, eliding others, syncopating here, clarifying there." In this spirit the speakers have prepared their talks for publication. This has been done, it is hoped, with firm commitment to historical truth, key word of the Sacco-Vanzetti conference.

Introduction

This volume brings together papers and memorial tributes delivered by distinguished participants in the conference, Sacco-Vanzetti: Developments and Reconsiderations—1979, which was held at the Boston Public Library on October 26 and 27, 1979. The conference was sponsored by the Library on the occasion of the formal presentation of the Felicani Collection of Sacco-Vanzetti materials to the Library by Anteo and Arthur Felicani.

At that time the two brothers gave to the Boston Public Library a major archival resource collected by their father, Aldino Felicani. Aldino Felicani was born on March 15, 1891 in the small Tuscan hill town of Vicchio nel Mugello. In 1914 he was forced to flee Italy because of his anti-militarist activities against the Italian government as a printer and editor of the newspaper *Rompete Le File* (Break Ranks) in Bologna. Felicani came to America where he continued his activities as editor, printer, and militant anarchist, first in Cleveland (*La Gioventú Libertaria*, 1914), then in New York City (*La Questione Sociale*, 1914–16).

In 1918 Felicani moved to Boston. Here he met Bartolomeo Vanzetti, his great friend, with whom he was preparing to publish a new anarchist journal, *Cara Compagna*. Their plans to publish came to a halt with the arrest of Sacco and Vanzetti in 1920. In the agonizing seven-year struggle for the lives of his two comrades—a struggle which he continued after their deaths in an attempt to clear their names—Felicani played a central role as the treasurer of the Defense Committee. He continued to print journals of anarchist propaganda during the defense of Sacco and Vanzetti (*L'Agitazione*, 1920–1925, and the *Official Bulletin of the Defense Committee*, 1925–1928) and later with the anti-fascist journals, *The Lantern*,

1927–1929, *Countercurrent*, 1938–1951, and finally *Contracorrente*, 1957–1967. In the midst of preparations for leaving his collection of Sacco-Vanzetti materials to the Boston Public Library Aldino Felicani died on April 20, 1967. It remained for his sons Anteo and Arthur to complete the final details of donating their father's collection to the Boston Public Library several years later—a gift which paved the way for the Sacco-Vanzetti conference, here recorded.

To supplement the materials in the Felicani Collection, an oral history project was begun by Francis Moloney, Assistant Director of the Library. While working on this project, he met Robert D'Attilio, who had just commenced his own Sacco-Vanzetti research. During the interval before the Felicani Collection was formally donated to the Boston Public Library the two collaborated closely, interviewing people and collecting additional Sacco-Vanzetti materials. Through their efforts the Library cooperated with the American-Italian Historical Association in a conference in the North End of Boston on November 11, 1972. Titled "Italian American Radicalism: Old World Origins and New World Developments," the conference featured a special session on the Sacco-Vanzetti case.

Under the aegis of the Boston Public Library, Mr. D'Attilio's research, both in this country and in Europe, was assisted in part by grants from the Massachusetts Council for the Arts and the Humanities and the Olivetti Foundation of Boston.

When the details concerning the donation of the Felicani Collection to the Boston Public Library were completed, Francis Moloney, Robert D'Attilio, and I worked together to prepare the Sacco-Vanzetti Conference, held to mark the occasion and here recorded in *Proceedings.* Mr. D'Attilio has prepared the Chronology which is found in Appendix A, has selected the illustrations, and — with Jane Manthorne, the Library's Staff Officer for Special Projects — is responsible for the editing of this volume.

Aldino Felicani's approach to collecting the archive is vividly described by Norman DiGiovanni in these *Proceedings,* so I shall not repeat that remarkable saga here. As for the dimensions of the Felicani Archive and its implications for researchers, the assessment by Prof. Louis Joughin is most astute. After a brief examination of the papers he suggested that the material embraces the following: a legal case; American legal history; law in relation to society; aspects of local, regional, and national communities;

the sociology of institutions; the sociology of small groups; the particular ethos and operational history of the Sacco-Vanzetti Defense Committee; anarchism as a permeating force; the nature of three important men—Sacco, Vanzetti, and Felicani; and the derivative responses to the case in literature, art, and music.

In the years to come the archive as a resource will surely emerge impressively as scholars continue to study the lives and era of Sacco and Vanzetti in the areas which Professor Joughin has so perceptively delineated. The Boston Public Library is proud to be the focal point for such research.

Philip J. McNiff
Director

Sacco-Vanzetti:
The Legal and Social Aspects

Opening Remarks

Philip J. McNiff, Director
Boston Public Library

Good afternoon. It's a pleasure to welcome you all here this afternoon to help us open a conference which is celebrating the occasion of the acquisition of the important Felicani Collection of Sacco-Vanzetti materials to the Boston Public Library. It seemed to us that the importance of the material itself, as well as the significance of this landmark case in Massachusetts and United States judicial history, was a fitting occasion for a conference which would bring together a number of scholars who could work with us in reassessing the historical information on this important case from an historical perspective.

I'm very grateful to all of the scholars who have agreed to come and participate and join with us on this occasion, and it is now my pleasure to present Professor Salomone from Rochester University, who will be the moderator of this afternoon's session. Professor Salomone.

Introductory Remarks

A. William Salomone
University of Rochester

Thank you so much. Mr. McNiff. Ladies and gentlemen, for the second time during the last decade I come to a conference which reappraises one of the most significant events in the history of the Twentieth Century. To say that I am honored by the opportunity to be here—honored, indeed, almost beyond proper expression. I want to give my thanks to Mr. McNiff —and the Trustees of the Boston Public Library— for his kindness, for his invitation, for his hospitality; to my good, indefatigable friend, Robert D'Attilio, the likes of whom, for his devotion to the reappraisal of the *Sacco-Vanzetti* case, no one will ever surpass. And, if I may, to the memory of a man I'd gotten to know through correspondence and I might say, also to love, Francis Moloney, who, as you know, together with his wife, was so senselessly and prematurely lost to us some time back. That we should be here this afternoon at this time, this year, in this city, under these auspices such as the conference enjoys, to reappraise and also (let us not be afraid to admit it) to continue to do homage to two — no, to three — exceptional Italian immigrants, who were joined by friendship and by a strong solidarity of an idea of freedom, of an ideal of justice, for which they were, as we know, unswervingly willing to live, to fight, to suffer, and to die, I say to do this is indeed, an extraordinary—almost a unique—honor.

Nicola Sacco, Bartolomeo Vanzetti, and Aldino Felicani now perhaps may seem to ring as the names of eponymous heroes in a ceaseless struggle...in an *impossible* struggle against the gods. But they were human beings—human, oh, so human indeed!—so that, in this moment of an ever-continuing drama we do well to look back again at what they did and what they stand for. In just a while, when I finish my few words here this very afternoon! three of the most perceptive students of this moment in the drama, if you like, will address themselves to fundamental issues, the spiritual, social and moral milieu, aspects of the creative, the literary mind as it reacted to the Case. And, as we know, when we look at our program, tomorrow morning and again tomorrow afternoon, a further attempt will be made on the part of other scholars, of other students, of other devotees to throw even further light upon this stupendous affair. Today's doings, and tomorrow morning and tomorrow afternoon's doings, will be linked by the events which will occur this evening. An important event, truly, where the children—Anteo and Arthur—the sons of Aldino Felicani, who was, perhaps without exaggeration, the most faithful, the most loyal, the staunchest, the irreplaceable friend of Sacco and Vanzetti, this evening will present the collection of their papers, their documents, their materials of their father to the Boston Public Library. And it seems to me that what we do this afternoon, what will be done tomorrow, and the fact that this kind of perennial gift will remain here for future scholars to dig into and to do what we are doing here this afternoon once again, is truly worthy of memory.

We shall be privileged to be at once participants and spectators, therefore, of a truly new moment in an old but unique drama. We shall be witnesses these two days to what is regarded as one of the most difficult challenges to the collective mind of all those, whether they be here or not with us, who, at one time or another have shown their humanity by their interest in the case of Sacco and Vanzetti. To me it seems that at the heart of that collective challenge to the mind lies the attempt that will certainly be made here to square a circle, to square the circle — the circle that continues paradoxically to elude us in our understanding and to be fragmented, to taunt us to understand, to know more, and that appears to be polarized, in which there is a kaleidoscopic succession in the books, in the pamphlets, in the materials — some of which are on display here. We view the variety of images, of visions, of judgments of the tragedy of Sacco and Vanzetti. We (at least, we historians) attempt to place that tragedy in some kind of perspective. Always that tragedy appears torn between images, at the heart of which was Nicola Sacco's and Bartolomeo Vanzetti's ideology of freedom, and a counterpolitics of official fear and oppression. For we remain ever painfully suspended between the desire to extract rational understanding and the passion of intellectual, moral, and spiritual commitment for us to know the whole truth. In a word, our irresistible *engagement*, if I may so put it, is to want to square that circle, which is constituted, in my mind, by the polarization, by the tension, by the conflict very often, in the literature on this case, by the documents, between history and biography, between objectivity and personality, between certainty and opinion, between contemplative sympathy and activistic passion, as we journey into the interior of this drama without equal...concerning two, three, I say, human beings, three lives who certainly gave assent to the human struggle itself. Far be it for me to suggest that the time has come, or will come, or should come when the so-called "affair" or the case will become depersonalized. God only knows what the depersonalization has meant to those who make living history today, to the millions of the voiceless, the disinherited, the hopeless victims of a soulless and mechanized civilization. And most of us know only too well that in our world, for millions of men and women of all races and colors and creeds and aspirations, depersonalization — be it actual or historical — depersonalization has meant only the eradication, the elimination, the dehumanization of life. And this was exactly the kind of new barbarism, of new roads to enslavement of the human personality, that Sacco and Vanzetti fought against. But there need be no contradiction between the search for historical truth, it seems to me, and the creative compassion that begets an act of commitment to human solidarity. Love, if I may say so, is not an adversary, but the companion, of truth. I believe that our gifted, expert speakers here today — even if they should not help us to fully square that circle to which I referred as the square of paradoxes — will certainly throw great light, will certainly illumine our paths, if we meditate on their words: words opening up the darkest spot of that *"gran selva oscura"* (great dark forest) which continues to be the Sacco-Vanzetti case. And we shall be ever grateful to Anteo and Arthur Felicani for making accessible from today on at the Boston Public Library their precious collection. We hope that study of it may lead to deeper, fuller, richer understanding of what made Sacco and Vanzetti and Aldino Felicani the men, the extraordinary models of human dignity they were — three unheroic but gigantic fighters for justice and freedom — men unbroken by social calamity and judicial prejudice.

4

Louis Joughin, Historian

Beyond Guilt or Innocence; The Responsibility of History

Many Americans, moved by curiosity or by moral sensitivity, have for more than fifty years asked students of the Sacco-Vanzetti case: "Do you think the men were guilty or innocent?" This challengingly simple query cannot, however, be truly answered. For two reasons. First, the question does not engage accurately with the central decisions of the case at law. Second, it does not confront that greater case in which the adversaries were the conscience of mankind and the maladministration of justice. Additionally, the question of guilt or innocence can rather easily become an exercise in antiquarian speculation. That kind of study too often diverts us from our humanistic and pragmatic obligation to look into the past in order that we may do better in the present and the future.

1. Guilty or innocent

The too-simple question, guilty or innocent, can at least be recast to meet squarely the judgments announced in the courtrooms. Thus, in expanded terms: did the Sacco-Vanzetti jury, as it began its deliberations on July 14, 1921, have before it as complete a body of evidence as was then available, had this evidence been fairly presented, and had the accused been adequately defended? We now know that these standards were not met; the Dedham trial lacked important available evidence, was in several respects patently dishonest, and often reveals a feeble defense. We do not know whether the jury was aware of these deficiencies. But a reading of the *Transcript of the Record* clearly indicates the existence of a formidable barrier of doubt which was not surmounted.

Between 1921 and 1927, additional important information was discovered and offered by the defense for testing by trial. This new material should, by any standard of justice, have led Judge Thayer and the Supreme Judicial Court to order a new trial, but that was not done. Unbelievably, the high court fell back upon its established position: "It is not imperative that a new trial be granted, even though the evidence is newly discovered, and if presented to a jury would justify a different verdict." This pronouncement was offered despite the fact that in this capital case reasonable doubt had become massive and on several issues preponderant.

Second, with the passage of time it has become certain that some of the individuals responsible for the structuring, prosecution, and adjudication of the case against Sacco and Vanzetti performed their duties in such fashion as to injure severely the reputation of the Commonwealth for even-handed dispensation of justice. Inevitably, over half a century the matter of guilt or innocence became subordinate to a larger issue, the need to determine why one of the major centers of civilization should have failed so signally to be just.

For that long span of time, it must suffice to give the views of two students of the case, one writing in 1927 and one in 1977.

The first is Bartolomeo Vanzetti, writing a few hours before his death in the electric chair:

What I wish more than all in this last hour of agony is that our case and our fate may be understood in their real being and serve as a tremendous lesson to the forces of freedom — so that our suffering and death will not have been in vain.

5

The second is Michael S. Dukakis, governor of the Commonwealth of Massachusetts, in his proclamation of July 19, 1977:

WHEREAS: The conduct of many of the officials involved in this case shed serious doubt on their willingness and ability to conduct the prosecution and trial of Sacco and Vanzetti fairly and impartially; and

. . . .

WHEREAS: The limited scope of appellate review then in effect did not allow a new trial to be ordered based on the prejudicial effect of the proceedings as a whole; and

. . . .

WHEREAS: The people of Massachusetts ... recognize that all human institutions are imperfect, that the possiblity of injustice is ever-present, and that the acknowledgment of fault, combined with resolve to do better, are signs of strength in a free society; and

. . . .

WHEREAS: Simple decency and compassion, as well as respect for truth and an enduring commitment to our nation's highest ideals, require that the fate of Nicola Sacco and Bar-tolomeo Vanzetti be pondered by all who cherish tolerance, justice and human understanding;

. . . .

NOW THEREFORE, I ... do hereby proclaim August 23, 1977, "NICOLA SACCO AND BARTOLOMEO VANZETTI MEMORIAL DAY"; and declare, further, that any stigma and disgrace should be forever removed from the names of Nicola Sacco and Bartolomeo Vanzetti, from the names of their families and descendants, and so, from the name of the Commonwealth of Massachusetts; and I hereby call upon all the people of Massachusetts to pause in their daily endeavors to reflect upon these tragic events, and draw from their historic lessons the resolve to prevent the forces of intolerance, fear and hatred from ever again uniting to overcome the rationality, wisdom, and fairness to which our legal system aspires.

Hence, in 1979, it is probably correct to say that the Sacco-Vanzetti case has arrived at a point of essentially firm opinion on the matter of guilt or innocence within its deficient context, and that the basic chronicle about the moral dilemma of society is reasonably complete. Although present views may require revision if weighty new evidence is discovered or if further significant insight is offered, the time is now ripe for history to determine whether it has a further responsibility to society in this matter on the basis of the existing materials.

2. The nature of history; who is in charge

The practice of history embraces the painstaking gathering of information and its arranging in mean-ingful order, the recognition of recurrent patterns, awareness of all relevant contexts, appropriate sen-sitivity to the attractive and repulsive qualities of known individuals, and much besides. But all of this adds up to little more than a checklist of operations which could serve equally well in other inquiries about life, from credit ratings to the writing of short stories.

Broadly but precisely, history is the stated opinion of the human race about its own experience. The breadth of this definition is obvious; it permits the inclusion of learned academic studies and the remi-niscences of sentimental senility; it accommodates to the invasive counterpoints of religion, skepticism, socio-biology, hedonism, and comic-strip heroics. And since the universe of history is extraordinarily various, so are historians. But the central function of history remains persistently identifiable as an unceasing appetite and habit; we look back in order to under-stand our experience.

Three aspects of the historical habit require special emphasis. To begin with, history differs from other modes of inquiry by its reliance upon that particular perspective which is provided by the passage of time. This does not mean that sequence and causality are the same thing, but it plainly suggests that the exist-ence of such a relationship must be considered. Sec-ond, history has been termed an appetite; indeed, in a very serious sense, it both expresses, and attempts to meet, a deep human need. History addresses itself to our fear of today and our terror as we draw near tomorrow.

The third aspect of history which demands special note is the identification of its practitioners. The range is indeed broad. At one end are all of us in our mere identity as retrospective creatures. At the other end are those pseudo-historians who betray the true function of history and use it to support opinions which are essentially unhistorical. History rejects the demagoguery of those who are determined to persuade at all costs: professional revolutionists and reactionaries; party line Communists, Fascists, Democrats, and Republicans; blatant New Englanders and similar Texans; combative Italians, Irish, and Yankees.

Then there is the gentle middle range embracing those persons whose concern with history is so deep that they make it their career and seek to earn their living by this mode of inquiry. Familiar sub-species include scholars, popular writers of fiction and non-fiction, and journalists. As is usual in human enterprise, they run from the incompetent and the dishonest to the bearers of light and the givers of strength.

Society, of course, has to decide who is to be in charge, who is to exercise the responsibility of leadership and emulation. This is not the occasion to deal with that question. There are a number of good tests available. Butterfield offers one when he observes that the historian "performs an act of self-emptying in order to seek the kind of truths which the evidence forces us to believe whether we like them or not."

This taxonomic interlude is near its end, but there is place for one further important and agreeable observation. Since 1927, history as an art and a science has greatly enlarged its power to investigate and its capacity to interpret. New ways of study have developed and several of these offer promise precisely for such matters as the Sacco-Vanzetti case. For example: (1) co-ordinate investigation by history and linguistic science of the changing use and meaning of words, (2) recourse to philosophical instrumentalism for the light it throws on changing patterns of group and individual action, (3) the relating of history to myth and symbol. An instance: it is an important historical fact that Sacco and Vanzetti have been called "Labor's Martyrs"; it is interesting, though less important, that the two men in odd moments so regarded themselves; but it is not true that Sacco and Vanzetti were Labor's Martyrs. Sacco was a well paid worker on excellent terms with his entrepreneurial employer; Vanzetti was an odd fellow who peddled fish. True, both men had played minor roles in fairly important

strikes, but their personal value system—and therefore presumably much of their motivation—was inseparable from their deep attachment to what they regarded as the gospel of anarchism, (4) the development of new techniques for collective biography, and (5) the use in harness of history and psychoanalysis; as Stuart Hughes puts it: "...in history as in psychoanalysis we may conclude that the path of the fuller understanding of the individual lies through the group and vice versa. In both cases, the explanation of motive runs from the single human being to others comparable to him, and then back to the individual once more. ... This reciprocal method is the ultimate concern that history and psychoanalysis share."

The final section of these remarks considers, within the definition given and the procedures described,

3. The responsibility of history in the continuing study of the Sacco-Vanzetti case

Exploration of this responsibility can both throw light on our present understanding of the case and indicate the degree to which Sacco-Vanzetti history, within its limits, may serve the felt need of humanity for guidance. Four topics will offer a framework for consideration of this view.

Traditional legal history. Some of the problems in this case are indeed old, and apparently in little danger of being solved. When *The Legacy of Sacco and Vanzetti* was first published in 1948, Edmund M. Morgan, the author of the legal chapters, bore down hard on the weaknesses of the adversary system, the misuse and non-use of experts, and the dim prospects of a defendant in a criminal action who was feared or hated by his community. Morgan was the Reporter for the *Model Code of Evidence* of the American Law Institute and consequently a chief authority in his field. But little has come of his adjuration; criminal law procedure has seen some improvement but it remains essentially a pitfall of random justice.

This writer recently prepared a list of eleven points in this case which embody the denial of due process, using categorical language which would free him from the identifying attributes of a particular cause. Then he read the decisions and opinions of the Massachusetts Supreme Judicial Court, from 1921 through 1927, which touched on due process in criminal proceedings; they were few. Then followed a reading of like decisions, for the same years, in the supreme courts of California, Illinois, and New York. Conclusions are not yet ready, but the effort is clearly worthwhile; it should provide a significant horizontal perspective. Ultimately, there will be a study of the same topic in the same jurisdictions for the 1970's, and thus a vertical perspective will be obtained. In this cross-comparison it will be particularly interesting, and perhaps revealing, to determine what influence *Commonwealth v. Sacco* has had in other courts.

Anyone turning to the Sacco-Vanzetti case for the first time in 1979 will find it almost impossible to believe that most federal Constitutional guarantees of due process seemingly had no force or application in the state courts of fifty years ago. For example, on August 20, 1927, Justice Oliver Wendell Holmes, Jr., in denying a stay of execution in this case, offered the following comment: "…as I put it to counsel, if the Constitution of Massachusetts had provided that a trial before a single judge should be final, without appeal, it would have been consistent with the Constitution of the United States. In such a case there would be no remedy for prejudice on the part of the judge except Executive Clemency."

Fortunately, we now have an excellent base for an historical study of the way in which, from 1941 on, and particularly in the Sixties, federal Constitutional protections, under the aegis of the Fourteenth Amendment, have become operative in some of the worst situations revealed by this case. Justice William O. Douglas, in a prefatory essay to the 1969 edition of the *Transcript of the Record*, reviews the decisions of the United States Supreme Court which now would prevent some important procedural injustices. The door is open to further significant study.

The curing of the faults observed in a famous case does not, of course, guarantee a new world of perfect justice. Any newspaper reader soon senses that in criminal proceedings it is still true that a damning accumulation of evidence of guilt is by its nature more conspicuous than a growing structure of reasonable doubt. And we still confront cases like *Stump v. Sparkman et vir* 435 U.S. 349 (1978), where the United States Supreme Court appears to discover no avenue for civil redress against a judge plainly guilty of permitting and condoning mayhem. Or, looking far into the future, one wonders when our courts will catch up with those elementary scientific principles which are used for arriving at conclusions

which are observed in our high school laboratories; there, fifteen-year-old adolescents learn that a deficient state of the evidence quite correctly precludes a final determination. Or one may nostalgically yearn for the antique Scotch verdict—neither "guilty" nor "not guilty" but simply "not proven."

Law as a social institution. It is a small jump over a meandering stream to pass from legal history to the study of law as an institution created by and serving society. For example, both law and the social matrix played their part in molding the small group of men who sat on the Massachusetts Supreme Court between 1921 and 1927. A reading of the memorial minutes adopted by their surviving colleagues discloses that six of the seven came from old New England stock, three of them from 17th century forebears; several had close connections with the mid-state area that Judge Thayer called home. Only one justice is exceptional; he was the son of an 1840 Irish immigrant.

Larger groups present larger problems. It is reasonable to assume that, in 1927, the members of the Boston bar took at least modest pride in their quality. How then does one account for the following 1928 judgment by one George R. Nutter:

> The Massachusetts Bar has been deteriorating for forty years and still is deteriorating. Its members are so "provincial" that they hardly are able "to see beyond the Hudson"…the laymen seem to accept defects in judicial procedure as an imposition of Providence with which they must be content. They see the almost religious adoration which the bar has toward the past, and they are inclined to agree that it must be sacrilege to change things which prevailed in 1850 under the regime of Chief Justice Shaw.…
>
> The Sacco-Vanzetti case showed serious imperfections in our methods of administering justice.

These are not the words of an irresponsible rabble-rouser or an angry anarchist; they are by the President of the Massachusetts Bar Association.

But history's warning must again be heard. The tenuous solidarity of large groups may indeed tell us little or nothing about any individual member.

Social change is obviously of prime interest to the historian because it involves the passage of time, but it is not always easy to account for. Consider the following extraordinary calendar of events. Sacco and Vanzetti were executed on August 23, 1927. The Massachusetts Judicial Council promptly began a study of the law governing appeals in capital cases. That Council, by the way, is an official body composed largely of senior judges, and in this instance the presiding person was a retired Chief Justice of the Commonwealth. Within three months the Council had formally recommended profound statutory changes. It proposed that a defendant's petition for a new trial would go directly to the full bench of the Supreme Judicial Court on the whole record of both facts and law. This recommendation was renewed in 1937 and 1938; it was made law by the state legislature only in 1939. Thus, we discover Council action within 90 days, and legislative enactment after twelve years! Indeed, a choice puzzle for an historian.

One further instance of the strange relations which sometimes develop between the law and society is the story of the Advisory Committee appointed by Governor Alvan T. Fuller in the Sacco-Vanzetti case. It was composed of the presidents of Harvard and M.I.T. and a retired probate judge. The duty of the group was not clearly defined, but in fact they were asked to advise the chief executive whether they thought the defendants to be guilty and whether there was a need for a new trial. An in-depth study of the work of the committee has just been completed; it is based on the existing record of its hearings, the committee report, and several newly available archival resources. A conclusion is reached that the work of this committee was at the very least incompetent.

Social forces and patterns in Massachusetts
in the Twenties and thereafter.

In the Sacco-Vanzetti case, as one would expect, an urban-suburban area with a long history going back to rural origins inevitably produced a great mix of values. Polarities, cohesions, and confusion abound. The murdered paymaster, Parmenter, came from an 18th century local family; his fellow victim, the guard, was the Italian Berardelli. A few months before Sacco and Vanzetti died, the first triple execution in the modern history of Massachusetts claimed the lives of three Irish boys; but James Byrne, then the only Irish and Catholic member of the Harvard Corporation, strongly opposed President Lowell's

conclusion that Sacco and Vanzetti were not entitled to a new trial. William G. Thompson, chairman of the Boston bar's ethics committee, and clearly a member of the region's core Establishment, gave almost the whole of his life for four years in service as chief counsel for the defense. Ironically, the district attorney, Frederick G. Katzmann, was attacked by the writer of a letter to a newspaper because his deviousness was characteristic of his "race"; the only difficulty with this barely concealed anti-Semitism is that Katzmann was in fact three-fourths a Scot and one-fourth a German. Such instances of the complexity of the Sacco-Vanzetti scene suggest that in this case our sense of history should be very much on the alert lest in passing judgment on individuals we fall into the quicksands of generalization.

A simliar caution is necessary when we deal with generalizations about regional habits of mind and value systems. The Boston area often prided itself on being out of touch with the world, but this of course is not true. Although Boston sometimes seemed to believe that the best kind of conservative tradition was that of practiced immobility, it also remembered that one of Massachusetts' claims to fame was Emerson's 1838 Divinity Hall speech. Similarly, although the metropolitan area looked uneasily upon evolutionary political thinking and skeptical habits of mind, it was simultaneously fostering the growth of such profoundly radical institutions as Harvard and M.I.T. It is true that strong ideological currents are found everywhere in the Sacco-Vanzetti scene, but they run in many directions and profoundly divert each other's expected courses. Historians, as well as judges, may need to postpone a verdict when the chief certainty of a situation is the dominance of uncertainty.

Reference has been made to the likely usefulness of combined historical investigation and linguistic analysis, of awareness of the role of religious forces in the development of social patterns, and of the great help which psychoanalysis may bring to the work of history. But just these three elements—people's words, religious feelings, and subconscious structure—can, when attached to established forms of historical study, result in inquisitive and interpretive processes of enormous complexity. We sense that we are only at the threshold of knowledge about the nature of human experience. So be it. The challenge, however, does at least permit the historian to dispose of the suggestion that the Sacco-Vanzetti case has really had its ultimate exploration.

There is time for two further illustrations of the inherent ironies of the case. First, there is Governor Alvan T. Fuller who used words in his career as a political leader, endorsed moral principles in almost religious terms, and somewhere within his subconscious reconciled the motivation needed to amass a considerable fortune and the equal inclination needed to render public service. We know that when the decision regarding executive clemency reached his desk he worked on his problem during many hours on many days. Taking it all together, the picture is admirable. But then one discovers that he is the same man who some years before, as a member of Congress, approved the denial of a seat to his colleague, Victor Berger, who had been elected by the people of Wisconsin, in these words:

> Berger characterizes the action of the House as a "crucifixion," and in a manner of speaking it is. It is the crucifixion of disloyalty, the nailing of sedition to the cross of free government, where the whole brood of anarchists, Bolshevists, I.W.W.'s may see and read a solemn warning.

Or take a quite different situation. The only point on which all Sacco-Vanzetti students are certain to agree is that their work could never be attempted, much less accomplished, if the *Transcript of the Record*, more than 6000 pages of it, had not been promptly published for all to see. Back of that considerable effort, as one would expect, there were expert editors and distinguished sponsors. But there were also costs. They were largely met by one man; he was an individual not given to many words or noted for "activism" in worthy causes, and these are important elements of negative historical evidence. He was, unlike Sacco and Vanzetti, deeply religious. In any event, the bill for the basic document in all the scholarship and history of the Sacco-Vanzetti case was largely paid by John D. Rockefeller, Jr.

Perhaps we are dealing with a new idea. The Sacco-Vanzetti case may be the kind of historical event which requires us to examine both the groups and the individuals involved in terms of their social literacy. An inquiry of this kind will obviously compel us to go beyond a mere bundling eclecticism and to develop a managed plan for the use of all the currently available approaches to human experience.

Personality in history. With all due respect for the focused history of armies, ideas, customs, and rulers, such works are inevitably derivative from that central stream which is composed of the individual experiences of all the participating human beings. So in the Sacco-Vanzetti case. There is obvious need for historical inquiry into the spirit and form of law, and into the institutions charged with the administration of justice. Also, it is important to study the actions of men in their official roles, even though the field of view may be narrow. Nevertheless, the ultimate probing must deal with Webster Thayer and Nicola Sacco, with Oliver Wendell Holmes, Jr. and Bartolomeo Vanzetti; these men constitute the prime evidence. In this matter, documentation affords some opportunity to get inside the human beings.

Read the Holmes-Laski correspondence. Be prepared for further material on Holmes which is only now surfacing. A supremely great judge, and an ardent patriot who in the defense of his country had been torn apart three times by enemy bullets. Also, perhaps, a somewhat cold nature not easily sensing or understanding the impact of injustice upon suffering victims.

Finally, consider Vanzetti.

Bartolomeo Vanzetti was born in 1888; his father was of very modest wealth, a small farmer; for reasons not yet clear the boy was apprenticed at age 13 to a baker. Under the stress of a work week which often approached 100 hours, Vanzetti in time became ill; at age 19 he returned to his home, soon to confront the death of a loved and perhaps idealized mother. In 1908 he arrived in the United States where he worked variously as a baker, dishwasher, frequently as a laborer, a cordage worker, and — eventually — as an ambulatory peddler of fish in the Italian colony of Plymouth, Massachusetts. He was arrested on May 5, 1920, at age 32. During the more than seven years he was in prison he continued his reading in history and philosophy, enlarged his command of English, and conducted a wide-ranging correspondence. Under the stresses he endured for so long a time, he was mentally disturbed for a period of a few weeks, and later for a day or two.

His ideology was at the same time simplistic and imaginatively illuminated; it centered around his concept of philanthropic anarchism. His manner of speech was both skeptical and humorous, and he often gently rebuked his admirers for their sentimentality.

Of Vanzetti's personal appetites and habits, we know that he was a hard worker, a lover of children and a delight to them. There is no significant clue to his sexual nature, although there is considerable evidence that his friends — men and women alike — loved him deeply. He was a person of simple tastes. There is no record of his ever having harmed anyone — except that he was convicted of murder.

What can history hope to do with a situation of such deep internal contradiction? The only responsible answer would seem to be for historians to commit themselves to ever deeper study, using improved instruments for understanding as they become available. Some possible steps toward such further study have here been outlined. In our efforts it is important that we remember that the primacy of the individual experience lies at the heart of the record of the human race. Thus, in the Sacco-Vanzetti case, put aside for the moment the issue of guilt or innocence; consider rather that after 83 months of imprisonment, Vanzetti made his extraordinary speech in the Dedham courtroom as he stood to be sentenced to death. Then unbelievably, one thing more.

After Vanzetti had concluded his statement, and as Judge Thayer began the imposition of sentence, Vanzetti tried to speak again, but was silenced. What on earth could have been on his mind? We happen to know; there is a document. He wanted to challenge Judge Thayer's revealed prejudice, but — far more important — he was remorseful for having forgotten to express his love and admiration for Sacco. The next day he wrote out his unuttered words; here are some of them. He is addressing Webster Thayer:

I have talk a great deal of myself but I even forgot to name Sacco...Sacco is a heart, a faith, a character, a man; a man lover of nature and mankind. ... Oh, yes, I may be more witful, as some have put it, I am a better babbler than he is. ... But Sacco's name will live in the hearts of the people and in their gratitude when Katzmann's and your names will be dispersed by time, when your name, his name, your laws, institutions, and your false god are but a deem rememoring of a cursed past in which man was wolf to the man....

. . . .

History goes on the best it can. Its practitioners, you may be sure, are ever grateful to and admirative of those who assist them to discharge their responsibility, as the Boston Public Library has done in establishing a focal point for the study of a major event in the life of this community and nation. In accumulating and sheltering Sacco-Vanzetti materials the Trustees and administrators of the Library have provided a physical and intellectual context for continuing inquiry into humanity's desire for justice.

The official record of the proceedings in the Sacco-Vanzetti case, and much of the analytical, historical, and critical commentary, is in print in 1979. The items here listed appear in the order of their first publication.

1927. Felix Frankfurter. The *case of Sacco and Vanzetti; a critical analysis for lawyers and laymen.* (Boston: Little, Brown, 1927.) New York: Grosset and Dunlap, 1962. With a new introduction by E. M. Morgan.

1928-
1929. *The Sacco-Vanzetti case; transcript of the record of the trial of Nicola Sacco and Bartolomeo Vanzetti in the courts of Massachusetts and subsequent proceedings, 1920–7* (paged continuously); *supplemental volume including Bridgewater case available materials* (paged separately). 5 + 1 volumes. (New York: Holt, 1928–9.) Mamaroneck: Paul P. Appel, Inc., 1969. With new court records at pp. 3732aa-tt and [525], "The Sacco-Vanzetti case—some forty years later" by Justice William O. Douglas, additional prefatory material, a chronology and a bibliography.

1928. Sacco, Nicola, and Bartolomeo Vanzetti. *The letters of Sacco and Vanzetti.* (New York: Viking, 1928.) New York: Octagon, 1971.

1931. Fraenkel, Osmond K. *The Sacco-Vanzetti case.* (New York: Knopf, 1931.) New York: Russell and Russell, 1969.

1948. Joughin, Louis, and Edmund M. Morgan. *The legacy of Sacco and Vanzetti.* (New York: Harcourt, 1948.) Princeton: Princeton University, 1978.

1960. Montgomery, Robert H. *Sacco-Vanzetti; the murder and the myth.* (New York: Devin-Adair, 1960.) New York: Western Islands, 1965.

1969. Ehrmann, Herbert B. *The case that will not die.* Boston: Little, Brown, 1969.

1977. Taylor, Daniel A. See the following item.

1977. Dukakis, Michael S. *The Commonwealth of Massachusetts, by His Excellency, Michael S. Dukakis, Governor, a proclamation.* Printed as an appendix to Upton Sinclair, *Boston* (1928), Cambridge, MA: Robert Bentley, 1978. This volume includes as a second appendix, Daniel A. Taylor (chief legal counsel to the governor), *Report to the governor.*

Barbara Miller Solomon, Harvard University

Brahmins and the Conscience of the Community

Anyone who has done research on the Sacco-Vanzetti case knows it to be an experience that stays in the memory, not to be abandoned. The innocence or guilt of the men, the lack of a fair trial, the motivations of the different individuals and groups involved with the case are matters that goad us still. When I was first asked to participate in this conference, the Lowell papers had just been opened. How could I refuse an opportunity to examine these papers? Earlier, I had made a study of the old New England elite, the "Brahmins," as they liked to call themselves, or the "Proper Bostonians," as others have called them. I viewed them in relation to the immigrants who transformed the region in the nineteenth and early twentieth centuries. In *Ancestors and Immigrants* I traced the growth of the immigration restrictionist movement among those Brahmins who subscribed to the notion of Anglo-Saxon racial superiority to justify an end to the free immigration policy of the United States. There was a Brahmin minority, I discovered, that upheld the older Yankee ideal of acceptance of strangers, of immigrants as potential American citizens. The restrictionist Brahmins, however, saw their belief in racial quotas incorporated in the federal legislation that excluded immigrants in 1921 and 1924. I discussed the Sacco-Vanzetti case briefly in the context of the full-blown racial prejudices of the 1920's, the period that really followed my study. With access to new sources, I would like to consider further the complexities and paradoxes in the Brahmins' social attitudes. As we all know, during the Sacco-Vanzetti ordeal many groups in the Boston community developed strong feelings about the case: Italian immigrants, middle-class Yankees, Boston Irish, as well as radicals from various ethnic groups

ranging from anarchists to national and international labor organizers. I shall focus my discussion on the reactions of the Brahmins, and show how these affected the outcome of the case and our understanding of it.

New England Brahmins formed the local gentry based on inherited status in old Yankee families, although some newcomers entered by way of marriage or talent. All regarded themselves, and were so perceived, as belonging to a privileged caste that carried the obligation to set the civic and ethical standards for the larger community. Brahmins, whether they lived in the city on Beacon or Marlborough Streets, or in the surrounding suburban towns, held a proprietary interest in Boston as the financial and cultural center of New England. By the twentieth century they were accustomed to the problems stemming from industrialization, urbanization, and immigration; but changing expectations in the democratic society called for new approaches to social issues. Philanthropies did not suffice in dealing with demands for equality and the elimination of poverty and privilege. While the majority of Brahmins opposed unions, the liberal-minded admitted the need for trade unionism for working men and women, and a few supported specific strikes. Brahmins divided as advocates and opponents of women's suffrage, making Boston a center for both positions in the pre-war years. Thus, in the Progressive Era, upper-class Bostonians ranged from conservative to radical; yet in the presidential election of 1912 relatively few of them were among the almost one million Americans who voted the Socialist ticket for Eugene Debs. And while more responded to the reform ethics of Woodrow Wilson or Theodore Roosevelt, most

Brahmins remained conservative Republicans of the William Howard Taft brand.

World War I intensified the strains in the Brahmins' accommodation of different social and political views among themselves as some opposed the United States' entry into the war and worked for an early peace. They found it increasingly difficult to agree on civil liberties for conscientious objectors, for Americans of German origin, and for other dissidents. The end of the war did not bring harmony; Boston was not immune from the national fever against foreigners. Tensions held in abeyance by the war erupted in urban industrial centers across the country. Boston had its clashes of radicals and police in the May Day riots. The nation's fear of Bolshevik agitators precipitated the Palmer Red Raids, and in Boston thousands of aliens were deported in 1919 and 1920. The low level of tolerance for differences in the educated portion of the community was evident when the Wellesley College Trustees "fired" Emily Greene Balch, a professor of economics, for her association with radicals in anti-war protests. Balch's Brahmin identity did not save her.

Also, in 1919, as Boston's economic prosperity waned in the post-war slump, the high expectations of local workers were frustrated by unemployment and inflation. A series of strikes began with the telephone operators and elevated railroad employees; then came the second massive strike of textile workers at Lawrence, reawakening fearful memories of 1912. Worst of all, Boston's model but poorly paid police force struck in the fall of 1919; the city became prey to mob violence before the National Guard took over. Shock of the citizens gave way to unforgiving rage at the strikers, and these policemen were never rehired. Most Bostonians did not know of Police Commissioner Curtis' arbitrary dealing with the request of the policemen to be affiliated with an A. F. of L. union, and that Curtis deliberately ignored a compromise plan, worked out by Mayor Peters and a commission chaired by the liberal Brahmin, James P. Storrow. This plan might have prevented that terrible strike.

I think of these crises as a prelude in many ways to the Sacco-Vanzetti case. While conservative Bostonians concluded that the policemen had gone "Bolshevik-mad" (I think Henry Cabot Lodge used that word), the small group of liberal Brahmins saw in the police strike a breakdown in communication among different parts of the community. John Codman, Elizabeth Glendower Evans, and Margaret Shurtleff led the League for Democratic Action, an independent public forum where all sides in labor conflicts could air their views. These same individuals, with other like-minded Bostonians, started the New England Civil Liberties Union and, in 1920, their Community Church for non-sectarian worship.

Soon a new and complex case claimed the attention of these liberal elements. On May 5, 1920, two Italian immigrants, anarchists, were arrested while sitting on a streetcar — one a shoe worker and the other a fish peddler. Many sources say that the men assumed that they were being picked up in one of the Palmer raids as radicals who had gone to Mexico to avoid the draft during World War I. Their appeal for help to anarchists and labor friends was answered quickly, with Aldino Felicani starting the Sacco-Vanzetti Defense Committee the very next day. A month later the arrested men were charged with murder.

Sympathetic Brahmins began to watch carefully. The trial a year later, from May to July 1921, crowded the Dedham courtroom with observers, and the dominant figure among many women was Elizabeth Glendower Evans. For the next seven years while labor radicals publicized the trial and appealed to their constituencies, Mrs. Evans became the important link between the anarchists of the Sacco-Vanzetti Defense Committee and the liberal sympathizers in Boston. She was generous in helping the Sacco-Vanzetti Defense Committee with financial donations, even though, as Felicani remembered, she did not always agree with its tactics. What made her capable of cooperating with people so different in political and social background and outlook? A glimpse of her past activities explains her dedication.

By 1920 Elizabeth Glendower Evans was a seasoned campaigner in many progressive reforms. The roots of her involvement lay in the unusual, informal education which had taken her out of the parochial confines of Beacon Hill to seek an understanding of the needs of unprivileged Americans. Born Elizabeth Gardiner in 1856, she had the conservative upbringing appropriate for a Brahmin girl, somewhat modified by the genteel shabbiness she and her mother endured as poor relations in the prominent Gardiner and Perkins clans. Still, she did attend private schools with her peers, and learned early to help in traditional charity work. She joined Phillips Brooks' liberal congregation and thought of becoming a missionary before she met Glendower Evans. Her future husband was a wealthy outsider from Pennsylvania, but a rebel by his family's standards for attending Harvard College. He later graduated from Harvard Law School and clerked for Oliver Wendell Holmes, Jr. After their marriage in 1882 this serious young woman absorbed her husband's ways of thinking about religion and society. Despite his death just four years later, Elizabeth Glendower Evans, as she chose to be called, carried out his expectations for her, first by becoming a trustee of the Massachusetts State Reform Schools and then as an innovator in prison reform.

Her husband's close friends, William James and Louis Brandeis, became her intellectual and personal mentors. At Radcliffe as a special student in the 1890's, she studied with Josiah Royce and Hugo Munsterberg; but later Mrs. Evans said that if she had to be on a desert island, her preferred reading would be Ralph Waldo Emerson's essays.

The Spanish-American War of 1898 evoked Evans' first feelings of opposition to the prevailing United States foreign policy. Like William James, she was an anti-imperialist. A decade later she turned to concrete social questions and, at Brandeis's urging, went to England to study trade unionism. Upon her return the next year, her education advanced in unanticipated ways. A Bryn Mawr social activist asked her to go to a suffrage lecture and she attended reluctantly; and when the next day somebody else called and asked her to speak about suffrage to immigrant women at factory doors, Evans hesitated again. She was not yet a believer in women's suffrage, but she went and found to her surprise that she liked taking the trolley to the factory and talking with working women. The experience taught her the importance of the vote for women as a means of improving conditions for workers. Her activities also led to an enlightening visit with the Robert LaFollettes in Wisconsin, who introduced her to midwestern social activism.

After these exposures Evans focused on the problems of working-class people and soon led the Massachusetts crusade which produced the first minimum-wage legislation for women in the United States. Through the Women's Trade Union League she picketed at a strike of weavers in Roxbury in 1910 and became active in Lawrence in 1912 and 1919

even though she owned stock in these factories. Relating one of her encounters to Belle LaFollette, she wrote about a conversation with an old Italian who still wore proudly his Garibaldi button: "I smiled at him and he smiled back and without words we began to communicate. . . . For thirteen years he has worked as a spinner in a cotton mill; and I supposed, been spurned as a 'Dago.'" Still Evans had the faith of an optimistic reformer.

The start of World War I in 1914 jolted her vision, and soon she joined an extraordinary group of American women who went with Jane Addams to the Hague Conference in 1915 to consider, with European women leaders, how to work for an early peace. Though Evans admired President Woodrow Wilson, she opposed conscription and gave only reluctant support to America's entrance into war. But after the war she still maintained a personal relationship with Wilson and wrote to him in 1921 that she was "chagrined, yes, how wounded I am at your refusal to pardon Eugene V. Debs, a man of stainless character, imprisoned for a long term because he expressed his belief that war, all war, is contrary to Christ's command, expressing what he and practically everyone, at that time, believed to be a right of free speech guaranteed by the Constitution. ". . . For all time, Mr. President, it will be remembered, along with your splendid enunciations, that Debs was jailed in your administration, and that two years after the war was over, you denied his pardon. Alas. Alas."

Retrospectively, we see the Sacco-Vanzetti case touched on all the issues that Elizabeth Glendower Evans had thought about since the 1880's. The case encompassed the rights of prisoners, laborers, immigrants, radicals, women, and conscientious objectors. And it was a murder case involving civil liberties. Elizabeth Glendower Evans played a critical role in bringing its issues to the attention of other Bostonians, for she enlisted the support of influential Brahmins and publicized the trial by her very presence and in her writings. Her numerous articles in *LaFollettes Magazine, Survey, Unity,* and other periodicals analyzed the case with emphasis on the prejudices of the court. Evans portrayed Nicola Sacco, Bartolomeo Vanzetti, and their families in their everyday lives as sympathetic human beings caught in a web of circumstance during the Red Raids.

The Sacco-Vanzetti case divided New England

Brahmins in three generations at least. To this day some families recall that members differed so that they agreed not to talk about it. The case became a testing ground for the values of the New England elite and their allies among educated professionals and reformers: between those who upheld the old order in its legal framework and those who sought to transcend its limitations to prevent a potential miscarriage of justice. Evans drew many women into the case who, after attending the trial or studying the transcripts, were convinced that Sacco and Vanzetti did not have a fair trial. Those women who became well acquainted with the prisoners over the seven years eventually believed in their innocence. Some were Boston Brahmins and some were not, but all held Mrs. Evans in high esteem. Their sustained interest in the trial and their impressions of the case reached friends, neighbors, and relatives, and beyond into the larger community — and even to the women's colleges. They were leaders in women's organizations, in charities, in settlements and church groups who knew each other from work for labor, peace, and civil liberties. They were of different ages, many in their forties, twenty or twenty-five years younger than the vigorous sixty-five-year-old Elizabeth Glendower Evans and her impressive contemporary, Alice Stone Blackwell. Blackwell was the editor of *The Woman's Journal,* a friend of the Armenians in Boston and a socialist more radical than her mother, Lucy Stone, the nineteenth-century abolitionist and pioneer for women's rights.

Many of the inner Brahmin circle of Bostonians (to use Helen Howe's phrase) who felt intensely about the case, expressed themselves in private. The most visibly active for the defendants were associated with the League for Democratic Action: Margaret Shurtleff, mother of six children, a tennis champion, once a student at MIT, wife of a Boston city planner; and Katharine Bowdich Codman, president of the District Nursing Association and wife of Dr. Ernest Codman, a distinguished surgeon, who shared the openmindedness of his wife and of his cousin, John Codman. Other followers of this trial were Bostonians by adoption. One was a friend of the Codmans, Dr. Alice Hamilton, a midwesterner, eminent toxicologist, pioneer in industrial medicine, and the only woman on the faculty of the Harvard Medical School. She, who had worked closely with Italians at Hull House for twenty-two years, remarked that she knew "like-minded foreigners" who were anarchists, disillusioned with America like Nicola Sacco and Bartolomeo Vanzetti. Another believer was Jessica Henderson, a former businesswoman who had been jailed in 1919 with her daughter for picketing on the Boston Common during a parade in honor of President Woodrow Wilson, because the Nineteenth Amendment had not yet been passed. She was a pacifist and, at the time of the trial, a member of the feminist Woman's Party and head of the Anti-Vivisection Society. Also closely involved were Gertrude Winslow, secretary of the Community Church, and two other civil libertarians, Cerise Carmen Jack, wife of a Harvard professor, and her friend, Virginia MacMechan.

The prisoners' English improved, Vanzetti's more than Sacco's, because of language lessons given by Mrs. Jack and Mrs. MacMechan. The letters in the collection edited by Marian Frankfurter and Gardiner Jackson show that Sacco and Vanzetti, given books of American history, philosophy, and literature, tried to understand them. They never abandoned their own principles of anarchism, but could share with Evans and Blackwell one American hero, Eugene Debs. Vanzetti also found an anarchist element in Emerson which he enjoyed. The men showed love for families and affection for friends, including these women who were helping them. The prisoners' courage as they awaited execution communicated innocence to visitors. Those who came to know Sacco and Vanzetti could not think of them as cold-blooded murderers (unlike A. Lawrence Lowell).

Throughout the seven terrible years the women helped Sacco's family survive and tried to bring some measure of comfort to the prisoners, isolated from each other in separate jails for most of the period. We glean from the prisoners' letters that the women brought fruit, flowers, and books, to which Sacco and Vanzetti responded with warmth and enthusiasm. The women seemed to be free, although I cannot be certain, of a patronizing manner in their thoughtful attentions. In a draft of a letter to Sacco, Margaret Shurtleff noted that she was having some success in teaching his young son, Dante, to swim and expressed confidence that his daughter, "the little Ines," would soon learn.

Jessica Henderson traveled with her daughters to Italy in 1923 to reassure the families of Sacco and Vanzetti that they were innocent and would surely be freed very soon. Henderson reported to Evans that she had accepted a glass of wine at the Vanzettis' and experienced no difficulty with her temperance conscience. In 1927 Gertrude Winslow made the same trip but could no longer express optimism to the anxious relatives on whom she called. Finally, Jessica Henderson, knowing how much Vanzetti wanted to see his sister Luigia before he died, brought her to Boston. Without consulting anyone, she hired a car and took the grieving Miss Vanzetti to call on Cardinal O'Connell and he, though not forewarned, invited them in for tea and prayed with them.

These women, despite their good works, have received an unfair share of criticism for their actions. Some writers have used traditional stereotypes of women to reduce these supporters of Sacco and Vanzetti to mere sentimentalists. Others use descriptive terms in their writing, like "elderly" and "white-haired" to devalue them and, in doing so, discredit their opinions in this controversial case. An early example of this judgment appeared in a letter of the Chief Justice of the Supreme Court, William Howard Taft, written to Harvard's President Lowell (October 1927) blaming propaganda "created by large money contributions of female [*he puts female first*] and male misled enthusiasts" in keeping the case alive. In this context, Professor Arthur M. Schlesinger, Sr., rebuked the editor of *The Boston Globe* for its commentary in 1959 belittling "so-called" liberals and "sob sisters." A welcome contrast was Herbert Ehrmann's dedication in 1969 of his last book, *The Case That Will Not Die*: "to those gallant women who faithfully tended the flickering flame of New England idealism from 1920 to 1927."

It was not difficult for these women, who were not trained lawyers, to recognize the prejudiced tactics of Judge Thayer and District Attorney Katzmann. The judge was well aware of the presence of the prominent women, and one day he called in Mrs. Lois Rantoul who was representing the Boston Federation of Churches. When he asked her what she thought of the trial, she answered that she had not heard "sufficient evidence to convince her that the defendants were guilty." He expressed surprise and annoyance, and assured her that she would "after hearing both the arguments and his charge...come to him feeling differently." When the judge interviewed her a second time, however, she stressed that the testimony of Sacco's employer, called by the defense, showed that Sacco had a good reputation with him. The judge brushed aside that remark, claiming that the employer Kelley had said elsewhere that "Sacco was an anarchist and that he couldn't do anything with him." But in the report she wrote for her organization, as well as an affidavit she filed in June 1926 and a statement for the Governor's Advisory Committee, Mrs. Rantoul stated that she had found the judge's remark "to be untrue."

The Boston Bar was not unaware of those questioning the fairness of the trial. Many leaders appeared to be "indifferent or hostile," according to Mrs. Evans, and some who became involved later tried to stay out of the case. William Thompson is the foremost example of one who, in 1921, refused to serve as counsel; reluctantly he entered the case two years later and became wholly absorbed in it. Thompson's transformed attitude toward the case, and finally toward Sacco and Vanzetti, was most movingly described by John Farwell Moors, himself a liberal Brahmin and a member of the Harvard Corporation. Of Thompson he said: "He was a strange person to be drawn into such a case. The two men, besides being anarchists, were 'slackers.'... No one could have been more unsympathetic with them on either count. He referred to them with scorn when their case first became prominent. With equal scorn he called their public utterances 'mush' and their motley array of supporters 'silly sentimentalists.'" But once he entered the case, he did not stop. He cared too much for the legality and "had vast respect for legal processes." While at first not convinced that Sacco and Vanzetti were innocent, he knew that they had not received a fair trial to which they were entitled. "It was the duty of the Commonwealth," he said, to provide such a trial. In the end, however, Thompson did believe strongly in the innocence of the men and "sat humbly in prison with Vanzetti, on the eve of the latter's execution, and listened to the condemned man as to a prophet or a saint." Thompson paid a price for his courageous dedication to the case. The brilliant lawyer, a Harvard *summa* who had married into the Boston elite, lost his clients, was snubbed at his club, and generally suffered from isolation.

While the Boston Bar looked the other way, the Brahmin minority of questioners was growing. One was the young historian, Samuel Eliot Morison, who wrote to Thompson, "When people like you are sacrificing everything, I can't refrain from sacrificing something....The execution of Sacco and Vanzetti would cry out against us for centuries to come just as the witchcraft executions have. These are dreadful days, and nights, especially for us who love justice rather than reputation — especially for you. God help us all."

As the Massachusetts Supreme Judicial Court considered the last appeal, increasing numbers in the Boston community became troubled about the criticisms of the legal process. At this time Felix Frankfurter, a young liberal professor at Harvard Law School who had also resisted getting involved, wrote a brilliant article which appeared in the *Atlantic Monthly.* He had long been aware of the case through the Brandeises. Eventually Frankfurter invited Mrs. Evans to tell his law school class about the case. Frankfurter's piece infuriated and "stung" the conscience of the Boston Bar, as Archibald MacLeish wrote, but it also forced the civic-minded men of good will to act. John Farwell Moors enlisted the help of Bishop William Lawrence, head of the Massachusetts Episcopal Diocese, who agreed to go in the company of respectable citizens (including Margaret Shurtleff and Dr. Alice Hamilton) to seek the intercession of the governor of the Commonwealth.

In the 1920's Brahmins held a variety of views encompassing a spectrum of social attitudes that were not mutually exclusive, but which could cause a collision or conflict of beliefs. The Sacco-Vanzetti case proved to be that kind of a conflict. If you believed that the men had not had a fair trial, what should be done about it? If the legal code of the state courts made it impossible to provide a retrial, what recourse was there to satisfy one's conscience and save the reputation of the Commonwealth? Responding to the protests of civic-minded citizens (some of whom did think that Sacco and Vanzetti were guilty), Governor Fuller did what was expected, and made an inquiry. The committee he appointed included Harvard President Lowell, MIT President Stratton, and the retired judge and man of letters, Robert Grant, who was an old pal of Lowell's. Although there was no chairman, Lowell dominated the review committee. Brahmins, irrespective of their views of the case, were pleased by the appointment of Lowell. John Farwell Moors spoke for all kinds of Bostonians when he said, "Now we can rest assured that justice will be done." Elizabeth Glendower Evans agreed, but Nicola

Sacco and Bartolomeo Vanzetti knew better.

On one level, Lowell had much in common with Mrs. Evans; both identified with their New England heritage, both upheld freedom of conscience and the obligation of the privileged to serve the public. As President of Harvard, Lowell saw himself, like Charles W. Eliot before him, as a public leader for the larger community of the nation. Lowell, never one to seek popularity, was highly regarded as an independent conservative. His record as a civil libertarian was strong. Though he had encouraged Harvard boys to volunteer their services during the policemen's strike, Lowell ignored alumni demands that Harold Laski, a visiting lecturer, be dismissed for supporting the strikers' side. At the same time he had refused to take action against Harvard Law Professor Zachariah Chafee for liberal interpretations in civil liberties cases related to the Red Raids. Again, during the furor over Frankfurter's article, Lowell squelched the Harvard Overseers who objected to the appearance of the article while the Supreme Judicial Court of Massachusetts was hearing the appeal for a new trial. President Lowell asked, "Would you have wanted Frankfurter to wait in expressing his views until the men were dead?"

Despite these examples of Lowell's fair-mindedness, those who knew his stand on other matters of public policy should have remembered that Lowell had some blind spots. In 1916 he opposed the appointment of Brandeis to the United States Supreme Court stating that Brandeis did not have the confidence of the Boston Bar. For years during his tenure as President of Harvard, Lowell served as national vice-president of the Immigration Restriction League. Like its founders, Lowell thought that America was threatened by the influx of southeastern European immigrants from "alien races." In the early Twenties Lowell upset liberal alumni of Harvard by proposing restrictive quotas for Jewish students and appalled Brahmins of Abolitionist tradition by his decision that the few black students should not live in the new freshmen halls. Lowell was not an easy person to categorize; he was never one to accept the opinions of others until he had made his own evaluation. He commented to a friend, after the Advisory Committee's report had been released, that he had had a very different conception of the case from reading Frankfurter's article than from what he learned at the hearings of the Advisory

Committee. Yet, to the surprise and disbelief of the lawyers for the defense, Lowell's conduct of the hearings of the committee lacked the impartiality and thoroughness expected of him. The Sacco and Vanzetti Defense Committee was particularly dismayed because the hearings were closed to the public and the press and only the report of the Advisory Committee, which Lowell wrote, was made public.

Admittedly, in the final report — and even more in an earlier version that Lowell drafted — the committee weighed heavily the circumstantial evidence against Sacco and Vanzetti. They acknowledged that the evidence against Vanzetti was thin. In the committee's hearings Lowell minimized or discredited the alibis provided by Italian witnesses. He later commented that Italians were always making alibis. Lowell's handling of Bosco and Guadagni's evidence about the banquet is a well known and shocking example of his prejudice.

Perhaps the Goddard ballistic tests made in early June unduly influenced Lowell so that he did not come to the hearings with an open mind. I would suggest that Lowell was indeed predisposed to find Sacco and Vanzetti guilty, and that the Goddard report only helped to strengthen his bias. And once Lowell made up his mind, he never doubted his own judgments. Thus, in this case, Lowell's conscious and unconscious prejudices about immigrants came into play. Later, John Farwell Moors, who remained a good friend of Lowell's, told Felix Frankfurter that "Lawrence Lowell was incapable of seeing that two wops could be right and the Yankee judiciary could be wrong."

In sum, the Advisory Committee report upheld the verdict of Judge Thayer's court and saw no evidence of prejudice in the behavior of the judge or of district attorney Katzmann. Private letters from Calvert Magruder, a young professor at Harvard Law School, to Lowell demonstrated cogently that the Report was oversimplified in its presentation of the case, and that it "failed to grapple with the real strength of the defendants' contentions." Most Bostonians, and most Americans, accepted Lowell's conclusions without question. His correspondence following the Report, though, showed the great division between those who believed that Sacco and Vanzetti had not had a fair trial and that the men were innocent, and those who denied both positions. For Brahmins, who had believed in the superiority of their own moral leadership, the case became tragic evidence of the inability of their leaders to perceive and to admit their own conscious and unconscious prejudices. The liberal Brahmins, particularly of the generation who had become adults just before World War I, were shocked by Lowell's conclusions. Catharine Huntington, later a noted theatrical producer and director, wrote to President Lowell in September, 1927, after the executions, that she and her brother Constant, a London publisher, and their Harvard friends had regarded Lowell as "representative of the best in New England." At the same time she enclosed a letter from her brother, not intended for President Lowell, but which she passed on that expressed their sense of betrayal. In part it said:

It is a terrible business and I cannot think of Boston and Massachusetts ... the places I care for most without a shudder. We are used to having America attacked but always before we have been unmoved, remaining proud of our country. But what can we say or feel when we read "For the first time in 150 years, the Stars and Stripes [has become] the symbol of oppression"?

In the last month before the execution, liberals throughout the United States and in England reacted like the Huntingtons. The case drew new advocates among literary men and women. However much the guardians of law and order tried to suppress the memory of Sacco and Vanzetti, they did not succeed; the case stayed alive. Elizabeth Glendower Evans, William Thompson, Aldino Felicani, Gardner Jackson, Herbert Ehrmann and others left their mark on the conscience of the community. Governor Fuller denied Sacco and Vanzetti the clemency the liberals sought, but fifty years later Massachusetts Governor Michael Dukakis, one of the sons of the new immigrants, issued a proclamation on behalf of Sacco and Vanzetti "to remove the stigma and disgrace from their names, their families, and their descendants." The proclamation could not reverse the record nor did it change the tragic implications of the sentencing and executions of Nicola Sacco and Bartolomeo Vanzetti. And there was still no resolution of the issues. The case continues to stir the conscience and sorely test deep-seated emotions of Bostonians in all parts of the community.

For us in the late twentieth century the significance

of the Sacco-Vanzetti case may be to serve as a reminder of our own vulnerabilities. Like earlier generations in the community we need to be wary of unconscious prejudices in making judgments in matters we do not fully understand.

Notes

In addition to the published and unpublished sources alluded to in the text, including the original transcripts of the trial, I have drawn on the large *corpus* of books and articles on the subject. Unless otherwise indicated, the quotations may be located in the Elizabeth Glendower Evans and the Alice Hamilton papers (Schlesinger Library, Radcliffe College); the A. Lawrence Lowell papers (Harvard University Archives); and the papers (privately held) of Jessica Henderson and Margaret Shurtleff. Other quotations are from Liva Baker, *Felix Frankfurter* (1969); *Felix Frankfurter Reminisces* (1960); Archibald MacLeish, "Felix Frankfurter: A Person of Faith" in Philip B. Kurland, ed., *The Supreme Court Review* (1966); Henry Yeomans, *Abbott Lawrence Lowell* (1948); and John F. Moors, "William G. Thompson," *Boston Transcript* (Sept. 14, 1935).

Other works of particular relevance for my focus include Aldino Felicani, "Memorial Talk on Elizabeth Glendower Evans" (Evans papers) and "Sacco and Vanzetti: A Memoir," *The Nation* (August 14, 1967); Geoffrey Blodgett, "Alice Stone Blackwell" and Paul C. Taylor, "Elizabeth Glendower Evans," *Notable American Women*, volume I (1971); Richard L. Lyons, "The Boston Police Strike of 1919," *New England Quarterly* (June 1947); and Louise L. Stevenson, "Women Anti-Suffragists in the 1915 Massachusetts Campaign," *New England Quarterly* (March 1979).

Other books that contributed in different ways to my interpretation include G. Louis Joughin and Edmund M. Morgan, *The Legacy of Sacco and Vanzetti* (1948); Helen Howe, *The Gentle Americans* (1965); and Francis Russell, *Tragedy in Dedham* (1962).

It was a special privilege to inteview Catherine Huntington, one of the great supporters of the cause. In addition, I wish to thank the many individuals who shared recollections or lent me personal materials belonging to family members identified with the case: Sara R. Ehrmann, Rene Henderson, Sarah S. Ingelfinger, Anita W. Magruder, Joan H. Shurcliff, Cornelia Wheeler, Leslie Winslow White, Richard Winslow, and Betty Jack Wirth. I appreciate also various kinds of help from Erika Chadbourn, Bert Hartry, Dorothy Healy, Carol Lasser, and Lincoln Robbins.

Daniel Aaron, Harvard University

The Idea of Boston: Some Literary Responses to the Sacco-Vanzetti Case

What I have to say can be considered a coda to the proceedings this afternoon. I'm going to be very short.

In the spring of 1928 Edmund Wilson wrote to his old college mate, John Peale Bishop, then living in France, that he'd been asked to write the history of the Sacco-Vanzetti case and that he might undertake the assignment. "I've been very interested in it," he told Bishop, "and think it is the most important and significant event which has happened in this country for some time. For a while this summer it stirred up things to their foundations and made one suddenly aware of much that goes on below the surface in people's minds, and in society in general, which one ordinarily disregards." Wilson referred to the case again in October of the same year. He had decided, he told Bishop, to give up the idea of writing a book on the affair—not because, as Bishop suggested, he'd be better employed doing something else, but because he hadn't directly involved himself in the case while it was going on, and because he was too lazy to do the research. He now believed, however, that it anatomized American life "with all its classes, professions and points of view and raised almost every fundamental question of our political and social system." And it did so dramatically:

"As Dos Passos said (he was writing to Bishop and quoting Dos Passos), 'it was during the last days before the executions, as if by some fairy-tale spell, all the different kinds of Americans, eminent and obscure, had suddenly, in a short sudden burst of intensified life, been compelled to reveal their true characters in a heightened, exaggerated form.'" Wilson's recognition of this fact, as his letter to Bishop implied, was a little belated. He had not left Provincetown when Dos Passos wired him two days before the execution to take part in the Boston demonstration to save the lives of Sacco and Vanzetti, but a few days before he had seen in the "dumb, unmobile, unthundering storm" about to descend on Boston Harbor "some great, blank, immovable menace, the blank menace not merely of some disaster to humanity, but of the negation of humanity itself." Like other writers of his age and class, the case came to signify the widening breach between himself and the comfortable people he had grown up with. He felt a growing conviction that the liberal ideas of his boss, Herbert Croly, editor of *The New Republic*, had been tested and found wanting.

Robert Morss Lovett, teacher, writer and critic, and with Wilson one of the contributing editors to Croly's magazine, had said as much in an article published in November 1927. I mention it here because it sums up pretty accurately the mood of the artists and writers directly or indirectly involved in the Sacco-Vanzetti case. According to Lovett, liberals had believed that the franchise in public education would give the majority the power—and the intelligence—to rule themselves. During World War I, the authorities suppressed and silenced opposition and, through "mendacious propaganda," induced the public to support arbitrary acts that contradicted the government's announced liberal objectives. The "execution of two obscure Radicals," Lovett wrote, shook "the Liberals' belief in working for equal justice at free institutions and the application of intelligence to correct the shortcomings of the system, and in the possibilities of educating public opinion and making its control effective over the instruments of government." And when, after the travesty of a trial, Lovett continued, the case was submitted to a committee "selected for their prominence in the intellectual life of the community," the fiasco was complete. Lowell's report, "in its ignorance, carelessness, inconsistency, bias, contempt for the persons concerned, and complacency toward institutions," dramatized what the radicals had been saying right along — that the majority of the middle class and upper classes were willing to subvert the law when they felt their interests were endangered." Lovett concluded: "It is no longer possible to deny the existence of Class War in the United States. ... Liberals will be compelled to choose between the arrayed classes."

The call to make a choice between the Thayers and Fullers and Lawrences of this world and the cause of the oppressed continued to be heard for at least a decade, and to be expressed in a variety of ways. But in my remarks today I should like to concentrate on some of the immediate responses to the Sacco-Vanzetti case, particularly as it affected the minds and hearts of some writers who were drawn to the great Boston drama. One has to be very tentative in assigning reasons why a particular artist or intellectual got involved in the case, or in measuring the consequences of this involvement. Announced motives and reasons are unreliable; and so are retrospective explanations. Suffice it to say for my purposes that the trial and execution of the "shoemaker" and the "fish peddler" was one of those morally complex and archetypal events that attract world attention and arouse powerful emotions.

Probably the most deeply engaged of all the writers, and the one who wrote the most extensively about Sacco and Vanzetti in articles, pamphlets, poetry, fiction and plays, was John Dos Passos. Upton Sinclair may have done as much or more research in the writing of *Boston* than Dos Passos did in *Facing the Chair,* but Dos Passos' feeling of identification with Italian and Portuguese immigrants antedated his concern for a particular miscarriage of justice. "In college and out," he wrote later, "I had personally felt the frustrations that came from being considered a Wop or a Guinea or a Greaser.... When we took up for Sacco and Vanzetti, we were taking up for a freedom of speech and for an evenhanded judicial system which would give the same treatment to poor men as to rich men, to greasy foreigners as to redblooded Americans."

Another observer-participant, who wrote an impressive account of her ideas and feelings during the last days of Sacco and Vanzetti, (and then reviewed this account many years later) was a 37-year-old writer — not ordinarily identified with the left — I mean Katharine Anne Porter. She had come to Boston, as she puts it, in her "reckless phase of a confirmed joiner in the fight for whatever relief oppressed humanity was fighting for," and to act on the teachings she had absorbed in her ethics and government courses. Along with a disparate group of authors and writers—Dos Passos, Dorothy Parker, Mike Gold, Lola Ridge, James Rorty, Paxton Hibben, Edna Millay, William Gropper, Grace Lumpkin, and others—she had stood outside the Charlestown Prison at midnight, August 22, 1927, waiting for the switch to be thrown. She describes her thoughts and emotions on that "night for perpetual remembrance and mourning," the hallucinatory atmosphere of the picket line, the shame of the aftermath. And although she was no innocent, no novice (for she had seen a good deal of brutality and betrayal as a watcher of the Mexican Revolution), she came to regard the trial of the two Italians after a lapse of time as sequels to the trials of Jesus, Joan of Arc, and the Moscow trials of 1937 "in which the victim was already condemned to death before the trial took place, and it *took* place only to cover up the real meaning: the accused was to be put to death."

Her wonderful account is full of comic and poignant episodes: a drunken Irish girl after the execution sings "the silly words to the claptrap tune in march time" (Porter is referring to those lines, "In the beauty of the lilies Christ was born across the sea" in "The Battle Hymn of the Republic") while the Communist sympathizers flinch, and their faces go sour; the nephew of Henry James bails out the pickets; society ladies, "those strangely innocent women," enlist "their altar societies, their card clubs, their literary roundtables, their music circles and their various charities in a campaign to save Sacco and Vanzetti," and with — and I like this phrase — "their indefinable air of eager sweetness and light" bring the money they've collected "in the endless, wittily devious ways of women's organizations." I don't think she was patronizing!

But even more valuable are the passages in which she thinks back after 50 years to those August days, no longer sure about the facts of whether Sacco and Vanzetti were guilty or not, but sure all the same, that "this event in Boston was one of the most portentous in the long death of civilization made by Europeans in the Western World." It was, in short, a wicked act, and symptomatic of the ills not yet discernible in 1927. Lola Ridge, the poet, spoke for all the deathwatchers when she said (after risking being trampled by Boston's mounted police): "We have lost something we shan't find again."

For Katharine Anne Porter, this most reprehensible abuse of legal power was an episode in the never-ending tragedy of humanity. Only for a moment did she feel the impulse to kill the oppressor, and that occurred the morning after the electrocutions, when she rode in the hotel elevator with several of the sleek gentlemen who might have sat for a Gropper cartoon or modeled for Ben Shahn. One of them said to another in "a cream-cheese voice, 'It is very pleasant to know we may expect things to settle down properly again.' And the others nodded with wise, smug, complacent faces." She resisted because she realized that her urge to do violence to her enemy was a kind of collaboration with this crime. But others less wise and less controlled took much satisfaction in committing mental murder in their verse and prose.

The collective target seems to have been Greater Boston, Yankee Boston primarily and the xenophobic segments of its population, especially what John Dos Passos called "the Right-thinking, Puritan-born Americans of Massachusetts," the descendants of witch-killers full of hatred "of the new, young, vigorous, unfamiliar forces" that were "relentlessly sweeping them onto the shelf." Dos Passos juxtaposed Dedham, "the perfect New England town" (standing for "Anglo-Saxon supremacy and the white man's burden") and "the ring of factory towns round Boston, among which Dedham itself sits primly disdainful like an old maid sitting in between two laborers in a trolley car." Joined with the Protestant, Republican, professional-men, Dedhamites, at least for the moment, were "the almost equally wealthy Irish Catholic element" who shared the Yankee hatred of "furriners," that is to say, the "wops, bohunks, polacks, honkies, dagos," the people who spoke broken English and did the work. The death of their counterparts, "the two men in grey prison clothes," as Dos Passos described Sacco and Vanzetti in his poem, "They Are Dead Now..." had "burned out the wind / the stale smell of Boston."

Much was made of the "legalized murder" in the "cradle of liberty" and the "Lynchers in Frockcoats," a paradox that evoked a great deal of heavy irony from the left propagandists. Mike Gold inveighed against Boston "Blood Lust" and the "well-dressed Boston mob," of the type that "lynched Lovejoy during the abolition days." These people, he scornfully predicted, wouldn't be deterred "from their lust of blood sacrifice—these faded aristocrats. They are too insane with fear and hatred of the new America" and will simply "decorate" their conspiracy with "Puritan legalities." Another likened Boston to a "stagnant pool with a Book of Etiquette beside it." It was invariably the "'good' people, the latter-day Puritans," Heywood Broun explained who contributed to "the world's harshest tribunals." James Rorty addressed the "Gentlemen of Massachusetts" in a series of imprecations: "Understand this, you bleak hearts, you grey imposters, you wisps, you half-born, death-elected."

But it took an expatriate, the unconventional and un-proletarian Harry Crosby, to deliver the most violent diatribe against Boston. I quote "A Target for Disgust," dedicated to Sacco and Vanzetti:

> I curse you Boston
>   City of Hypocrisy
>   City of flatulence
>   (with your constipated laws)
>   Unclean City
>   (with your atlantic monthlies
>   and your approaching change of life)
> I curse you
> in the name of Aknaton I curse you
> in the name of Rimbaud I curse you
> in the name of Van Gogh I curse you
> your belly is a nest of worms
> your breasts tubercular
> you have a falling of the womb
> you are an ulcer on the
>   face of earth
>   leprous
> hogs vomit when they approach you
>   City of stink-Stones
>   City of Dead Semen
> with your Longfellows and your Lowells
> there is no Aphrodisiac can revive you
>   it is too late
> too late for you to cleanse
> yourself with sun

Aphelion
City of Tea Rooms
Whose beverage is
the water of the Dead Sea
whose food is Salt Peter
    and the juices of cod
City of Invalids
City of Fetid Breath
Walled in by Shadow
    Sunless
your libraries are clogged
    with Pamphlets and Tracts
but of Ulysses
    you have none
but of Gertrude Stein
    you have none
but of Maldorors
    you have none
your Churches are crowded
    with Sabbatarians
but of Prophets
    you have none
but of Fanatics
    you have none
but of Sun-Gods
    you have none
you are an Abomination
    Unphallic City of Pulp
and I would rather defile a
    dead body than uncover
    your nakedness
and I would rather spill out
    my seed upon the ground
    than come near to you
and I would rather dwell
    in the volcanos of hell
than dwell in your midst
    City of Swan-Boats
    City of Frog-Ponds
you are an Abomination
a perpetual sore
a target for disgust
and in the name of
    the Sun
    and the Moon
    and the Stars
and in the name of the Mad Queen
    I curse you
Boston City of Hypocrisy

In this and other verse polemics, it wasn't the city that was being pilloried so much as an *idea* inexactly objectified as "Boston"—the fount of Puritanism as desiccated as E.E. Cummings' portrait of A. Lawrence Lowell (whom he described to Edmund Wilson as going "around everywhere with a little poodle, whose balls trail on the ground and make the letter H—that's what he's like."); the butt of jibes about book-banning; the place where readers of the *Evening Transcript* swayed in the breeze like a field of ripe corn. But by 1927, "Boston" was no longer a subject for Menckenian fun. Its gentility and stodginess had suddenly turned into something menacing.

Very little memorable fiction, and practically no verse of any lasting merit came out of the Sacco-Vanzetti affair—in part because it was used by partisans as a call to arms or as an outrage to inspire vindication and win converts. An anthology of poems about Sacco and Vanzetti, *America Arraigned*, as one unsympathetic critic pointed out, contained "the same old banal impressions, with the same epidemic of verbal photography, with the same eternal evocation of proletarian misery." The political radicals, he said, "were literary reactionaries," a judgment prophetic of future events in both the U.S.S.R. and the U.S.A. where the corruption of the Communist ideal might have been anticipated simply by reflecting on the sufficating language of the revolutionary movement.

The Sacco-Vanzetti case influenced the social opinions of writers and thinkers who *did* write memorably on other themes. Melvin Lansberg rightly notes its importance in shaping the interest in politics of Dos Passos and supplying him with a "a new impetus for his study in American society—its leaders, its myths, its ideologies, its sources of information." But Dos Passos' summons to tell and re-tell the story of martyrs, in "writing so fierce and accurate that it will sear through the pall of numb imbecility that we are again swaddled in after the few moments of sane awakening that followed the shock of executions"—this summons might have been addressed to himself for all the effect it had.

America did not forget Sacco and Vanzetti, as this meeting today testifies. But excepting two works, Upton Sinclair's *Boston* and Dos Passos' *U.S.A.*, little of much literary value has been written about them. We are still waiting for the prose writer or poet or dramatist who will illuminate those aspects of the case that transcend questions of technical guilt or non-guilt, the partisan skirmishes, the rage and sentimentality and hypocrisy that clouded it, and reveal its grandeur and profoundly tragic dimensions.

Philip J. McNiff

Thank you very much, Dan. Before closing this afternoon's opening session, I want to express appreciation to the four scholars who took part in this program. We are planning to publish the proceedings of the conference as a permanent documentation of the occasion.

It's always dangerous to introduce people in the audience, but there are two whom Barbara Solomon mentioned, and I wonder if Catharine Huntington is here. She's planning to come to one of the conferences; she's not able to attend them all. The other person, whom I know is here, is Mrs. Herbert Ehrmann, who did so much not only in the case of Sacco-Vanzetti, but in many good works and deeds in the whole Boston area over a long period of time. I wonder if you would stand up and take a bow, Mrs. Ehrmann. And the other person whom I'd like to stand and take a bow is Miss Vanzetti, who has come here from Italy to join us for this occasion.

Now, I declare this afternoon's session closed. I hope we'll see you this evening when we come back at 8:00 for the Felicani memorial.

Aldino Felicani (1891–1967): Memorial Tributes

On the occasion of the presentation of his Sacco-Vanzetti collection to the Boston Public Library by his sons

Introductory Remarks

Philip J. McNiff

This evening is the second program celebrating the Sacco-Vanzetti collection that was put together, conserved, and preserved by Aldino Felicani. This afternoon we had four eminent scholars talk about various aspects of the Sacco-Vanzetti case. This evening we are having an interim program that will pay tribute to Aldino Felicani before tomorrow's program, which will deal with other aspects of the Sacco-Vanzetti case: the anarchist connection in the morning and in the afternoon, a symposium, Sacco-Vanzetti Reconsiderations 1979.

Aldino Felicani was an extraordinary human being who not only was a close friend of both Sacco and Vanzetti, but played a very important role in preserving the documentation of the Defense Committee — as well as preserving a sense of the dignity of human beings in the modern world.

We are going to open the program this evening with a talk by a long-time associate of Aldino Felicani, Norman di Giovanni, historian, although he decries the appellation of historian, but one who is a literary historian, a lecturer and an important colleague and friend of Aldino Felicani. He describes himself as a writer and translator, principally of the work of Jorge Luis Borges. He is going to talk to us first about Aldino Felicani, the man and his collection. Mr. di Giovanni:

Norman Thomas di Giovanni

Aldino Felicani: The Man and His Collection

Aldino Felicani died some twelve years ago at the age of seventy-seven. I knew him, we were friends, during the last ten years of his life.

One day in the latter part of 1958, long after knowing about Felicani's connection with Sacco-Vanzetti and about his editorship of the anti-Fascist journal *Controcorrente* during the war years, I walked into his printing office on Milk Street to meet him and to present him with a copy of a magazine in which I had written a piece about Sacco and Vanzetti. I was in my middle twenties; Felicani must have been in his late sixties.

Felicani was impressive. He was a tall, big-boned man, with shaggy eyebrows and beautiful long, tapering fingers that he often used expressively, in a hypnotic way, to give further shape to his words or thoughts. Both by his looks and demeanor he commanded immediate attention. At the same time, his intelligence and passion leaped out to assault you, and altogether he seemed to me as full of life as anyone my own age. Felicani did not strike one then, not in those years, as old in any way. He glanced at my name in the copy of the *Nation* that I gave him, pronounced that it would be useful to him, and slipped it into a desk drawer, where another copy of the same issue already lay. I imagined that he had accepted my copy out of mere politeness; it was a while before I was to learn that he had acted out of habit—an old, ingrained habit of acquisitiveness.

At the time I lived only a few blocks away from Milk Street, in the North End. I went home quite elated after our first meeting and within a week returned to see Felicani a few more times. My credentials, I assume now, had been the right ones. I was Italian-American; my background, like Felicani's, was radical, atheist, and anti-Fascist; and, of course, I had begun to write about Sacco-Vanzetti. In a matter of a month or so I was meeting Felicani frequently for lunch at a cafeteria nearby the print shop, where we engaged in long, leisurely conversation about anarchist philosophy and polemics, ethics, the personality and character of Sacco and Vanzetti, the literature of the Sacco-Vanzetti case, Fascism and anti-Fascism, Italy, writers like Dos Passos and Elliot Paul (both of whom Felicani had known), Kropotkin, Luigi Galleani, Alexander Berkman, Emma Goldman, labor causes, the Palmer raids, and Felicani's own personal history.

What happened next was inevitable. Our conversations, growing and growing as they did, began to overlap some of Felicani's other activities. His printing business in these years was run almost completely by his two sons; and although he came into the office six days a week, Felicani spent most of his time there either conversing with visitors or overseeing the affairs and production of *Controcorrente*, which he had recently revived in a smaller format. The new *Controcorrente* was produced entirely in Italian. Without the urgent purpose of the earlier series, it was in the main backward-glancing and nostalgic. Its cost was nominally supported by voluntary contributions, not by normal subscriptions, but these contributions barely covered a quarter of the printing bill. *Controcorrente* was a toy, a hobby, a way of life, a *grip* on life for Felicani. His sons bore the burden of it stoically. I happened to be present once when Felicani and a bookkeeper were engaged in the menial and tedious work of wrapping, sorting, and mailing an issue of the magazine. I made myself useful by pitching in. After that, somehow, it was my business to be available every time an issue went out, which was six and later four times a year. Much later, when there was no longer a full-time bookkeeper and Felicani was in poor health, my helping hands became indispensable. I took over all the paperwork and details of the mailing, and when a number failed to be printed on time I marched up to Post Office Square and made excuses to the postal authorities. I also persuaded Felicani to issue the magazine as a quarterly, and I worked out an ironbound production schedule for him. By then correction and updating of the mailing list was my province; in the end, I pasted up dummy proofs, ran proofsheets up and down floors to the presses, and even—to relieve his sons—learned to feed the machines that folded and stitched the magazine.

I draw attention to these mundane activities in order to show that our friendship was more than casual and that it took place against a background of workaday events. In this way, over a period of years, Felicani and I came to know each other. Of course, there were as well the more glamorous, one-off enterprises that make good anecdotes and are colorful to look back on. Felicani had contributed to Columbia University's oral history program; and once, working from a transcription of that material, we wrote a chapter of his life that impressed the Atlantic Monthly Press enough to offer us a book contract. The chapter was published posthumously in the *Nation*. And one wintry morning, near the outset of our friendship, I found myself in the company of Catharine Huntington, an elegant Beacon Hill lady, and Felicani—just we three—in the highly unusual circumstance of picketing the Museum of Fine Arts. It seems that they were exhibiting a collection of Alvan Fuller's paintings, and Felicani could not let an opportunity like that pass without reminding the public that one of Governor Fuller's masterworks, thirty-two years earlier, had been the execution of Sacco and Vanzetti. We distributed a leaflet, which Felicani had had run off the day before, showing the death masks of the two anarchists. It was arranged for the press to be there, and that evening the *Boston Globe* ran a front-page story about our little demonstration. Felicani had staunch friends and useful connections, and I admired him for the way he knew how to get things done. Of course, a few days later I had to skulk back inside the museum to look at the Fuller pictures for background material for the piece I wrote about our escapade and that Irving Howe

eventually published in *Dissent*. It was Felicani who gave me its title, which was "The Missing Masterpiece."

And so two or three years passed. When the Boston winters got me down, I went to live and work in Puerto Rico, remaining there for a longish time. Felicani and I corresponded sporadically. Now it should be made clear that up until this time I knew that somewhere at the Excelsior Press Felicani had whatever files remained of the Sacco-Vanzetti Defense Committee. But in the early years of my association with him I don't think I ever saw a scrap of that collection, except for printed pamphlets—many of them old and extremely scarce — of which there were duplicates and of which Felicani often made gifts. I eagerly accepted whatever he gave me. Occasionally, upon my asking about some other published material, he went off alone into the heart of his six-floor building and returned with a copy for me. I never asked for more. I did not dare, because I did not want to be refused. Nobody except work staff was allowed unaccompanied into any part of the press. No writer researching for a book was ever shown anything but printed material. Nobody every caught a glimpse of the Felicani collection. All this was ironbound, and my closeness to Felicani gave me no special privileges. The man stood like a fortress between the outside world and the materials he had preserved, and I simply knew that there was no power on earth that was going to budge him—not yet.

During my two-and-a-half-year absence I thought in a fresh way about Sacco and Vanzetti, and when Carey McWilliams of the *Nation* got me a small research grant I came back to New England. Beforehand, however, through letters and a personal emissary, I told Felicani what I was up to, explained what I wanted, and got his word that he would open his collection to me. But now Felicani was a different man. Stooped and in ill health, he no longer went out for lunch but ate a frugal sandwich at his desk. He could not walk any appreciable distance, and in cold weather he had difficulty catching his breath. But he stubbornly refused ever to stay at home. Sometimes, bristling with impatience, he was unable to contain his temper and irritability. With the deaths of so many of his friends and contemporaries, suffering the animosity of certain of his old comrades over issues that were purely historical and otherwise entirely irrelevant, Felicani stood in isolation and loneliness. But he was cheered by my return, and this was when I became indispensable to him in getting out his magazine. We spent more time together now. I got more out of him about his life before he emigrated to America and about his early years here. Spurred by this, and with letters and contacts provided by him, I eventually visited the families of Vanzetti, in Piemonte, and Sacco, in Puglia, and Felicani's own birthplace, near Florence, and the town where he grew up near Bologna.

As for the collection and his revealing it to me — well, he hesitated and chafed and delayed for a couple of weeks. I realized that the reticence and instincts of many decades were not going to disappear overnight. I was patient. At last he got under way opening desk drawers in his office. The treasures began haphazardly to pour out. I remember handwritten letters and postcards (nobody typed in those days) from Vanzetti, in Plymouth, to Felicani, in Boston, some time before the events of Bridgewater and Braintree. Vanzetti and Felicani were trying to found a new anarchist publication. Vanzetti sent a manuscript, with characteristic apologies for its inadequacy. How on earth, why on earth, had these writings been preserved? One thing alone explained this and explained what I was about to stumble onto. Felicani saved everything — or, put another way, Felicani threw nothing away. This was both his virtue and his failing.

Felicani took great pleasure in my enthusiasm over these finds. I was collecting Vanzetti manuscripts from numerous other sources and putting together the pieces of a picture some of which Felicani himself did not know and a lot of which he had forgotten. Soon enough I was led by him to the inner sanctum. What I saw that day made my heart soar to the sky and sink down into my shoes — both at the same time. A corner of one of the floors had been partitioned off to make an office. A great deal of material was stored there, in filing cabinets, on top of filing cabinets, on shelves, on desks, on chairs, and about three feet high over every square inch of the floor. But, as yet, this room was inaccessible, for a mountain — literally — a pyramid of accumulated paper blocked the way. All this was the heart of the collection. When days later I had shifted a bit of the mountain to gain the door, it could not be pushed open for what lay on its other side. I simply could not believe my eyes. Felicani was enormously proud of what he had preserved and amassed; it was now obvious to me that he was also greatly ashamed of the condition the

material was in. His collection was legendary, but nobody knew the truth about it — that it stood in a most appalling shambles.

I don't know what I expected. Certainly not this. There was no beginning and no end to the material. As I felt my way and tried to open passageways, sifting, sorting, and discarding, Felicani sat by my side like a watchdog. Quite soon, however, he realized that this was hopelessly boring and a waste of his time, so he left me alone. I had to reconsider everything I had set out to do. Rescue was now the order of the day, and my first job was to survey the whole building in order to determine the extent of the sprawl. It turned out that we were to assemble valuable material from nooks and crannies on four of the building's six floors.

Felicani's sons were quick to recognize the double advantage of what I was doing — getting the material organized and freeing them of the clutter of it. One of them, Anteo, spent hours encouraging and offering me every kind of practical assistance, providing boxes, wrapping materials, labels, and brute strength. Together, he and I sorted out tumbled heaps of old issues of *Controcorrente*, which we made into sets and had bound, so that one of Felicani's most successful and most valuable undertakings was made complete and available for the first time.

Similarly, I was able to put together complete collections, for the first time, of the five periodicals — sixty-three issues in all — published by the Defense Committee between 1920 and 1930. And with Felicani there to have his memory stirred, I was able to establish why, for example, there were two different issues of the first number of a particular bulletin.

I spent part of each day reducing the bulk, trying to create much needed elbow-room and space, and another part ransacking the corners of the building and carrying boxfuls of preserved material to the vicinity of the inner sanctum. For disposal, I was provided with huge burlap sacks, the ones that the press's waste was collected in each week or so. How many hundreds of those we filled I no longer recall. The work went on month after month for four years — full-time at first, and toward the end, when the bulk was more manageable, two days a week.

What was in these mounds of paper? Old printing jobs; newspapers and magazines of every kind and description, a good many of which contained nothing of interest; files of business correspondence; Sacco-

Vanzetti files; Vanzetti manuscripts; old blotters; circulars from ink manufacturers, from paper manufacturers, from type founders—in short, anything and everything. And each item had to be inspected, turned over, examined, opened, unfolded. There was no accounting for what would turn up next to what. It was a treasure hunt. In winter the place was freezing; in summer, breathless. I was black with grime at the close of each day, for whatever I touched was thick with dust and dirt. At times I was unutterably bored. At times, to relieve the boredom, I would lock myself up, sort the treasures I had assembled, read them, absorb them, and make notes.

And so the process was repeated when we came to the inner office—the endless sorting and discarding, the endless parade of burlap sacks. By this time, having Felicani's complete trust, I was to destroy whatever I judged should be eliminated. He never specified; it was tacit. A good deal of personal correspondence, private correspondence, belonging to members of the old Defense Committee had somehow crept into the papers, and Felicani wanted it removed without wanting to know about it. Often when he came upstairs to see how I was getting on, I would pass him a letter and say, "This has nothing to do with Sacco and Vanzetti, does it?" He would glance at the handwriting or signature, go into a deep reverie, and shake his head no. He sometimes had his doubts about legitimate material as well—for instance, the financial records that he himself had so painstakingly watched over and assembled. He no longer saw the point of hanging on to such lifeless detail. But I did, and we kept them.

What, in the end, was preserved? What, in its present form, is the scope of the collection? Primarily it is the *corpus*, more or less complete, of the papers of Sacco-Vanzetti Defense Committee from its inception in 1920 to its demise around 1929. This embraces correspondence, notes, and materials of Fred Moore in preparation for the Dedham trial and subsequent legal investigations, amounting to several thousand pages. Then there are Moore's letters and appeals as director of publicity, as well as the records and correspondence of the committee when it was under Moore's direction. Then there are the papers of the committee after Moore's departure from the case, including the correspondence, organizational and tactical, with William Thompson and other defense lawyers, with nationwide Sacco-Vanzetti

conferences, and with the International Labor Defense. Then there are the legal records and documents, in typescript and printed volumes, together with affidavits, briefs, and supplementary motions. Then there are all the committee's publications: four complete serials, comprising sixty-three issues; every pamphlet and leaflet, every handbill and circular letter, every letterhead and other piece of stationery, every press release, and such pictorial material as lapel buttons, funeral armbands, picketing placards, and posters. Then there are volumes and volumes of mounted and unmounted press and periodical clippings and five volumes of publicity scrapbooks, containing handbills and leaflets, often annotated with dates and numbers of issue. There are at least nineteen manuscripts by Sacco, letters and articles, including the longest extant Sacco manuscript. There are over 150 English and Italian manuscripts by Vanzetti, some hundred or more letters and twenty articles, translations, literary compositions, notes, marginalia, various jottings, and fragments; much of this material is lengthy, and hitherto it was considered that many of these manuscripts were either lost or never existed (I'd like William Buckley to stick his nose into these and see whether he would continue to stand by his statement that the Sacco-Vanzetti letters were written by someone else.) There is even a most extraordinary love letter from Vanzetti to the woman who taught him English. There are a series of letters and other writings by Sacco and Vanzetti for which no autograph manuscripts are extant. There are the letters written to Sacco and Vanzetti. There are the committee's financial records: eighteen volumes of ledgers, typed reports, and notebooks; seven volumes of checkbooks and check stubs; and Fred Moore's checkbook with attached cancelled checks; and boxfuls of vouchers and receipts. (It must be remembered that Felicani not only founded the Defense Committee but served as its treasurer, and it was his greatest pride that, having collected tens of thousands of dollars, he never received a complaint from anyone that even a penny was unaccounted for.) Then there are the scores of photographs, some illustrating points of evidence and constituting legal documents. There are the death masks of Sacco and Vanzetti (the original ones, not the ones I have been accused of having in my private possession, which are copies that were presented to me twenty years ago by Gabriel Piemonte.) There are the ribbons with their mottoes from the floral pieces at the funeral. There are the items, such as beadwork and penholders, made by fellow prisoners and presented by Vanzetti to friends. There are the papers of the short-lived Sacco-Vanzetti New Trial League. There is a mass of material acquired by Felicani, including his own papers, since 1927. There are the papers of Elizabeth Glendower Evans, given to Felicani for safekeeping. And there are also papers of Fred Moore, prior to the Sacco-Vanzetti case, which are valuable for throwing light on Moore's methods of work and for showing his connections in labor and radical circles.

That this collection has survived and come down to us is owed to a series of minor miracles. Quite early, part of it was stolen, ending in the hands of the prosecution. Eventually, after the death of one of the assistant district attorneys, this was bequeathed to the Harvard Law Library. Another part of it was dispersed — this time for reasons of safekeeping — and was lodged at the Harvard Law Library, where it has remained for the last fifty years. And what we have today, what the Boston Public Library now holds, was through the years physically moved along with the premises of the Excelsior Press no fewer than three times, some of it by hand trucks over the rough, cobbled streets of the North End. And, of course, there is also the fact that Felicani, as a printer, had the space to keep such a vast amount of material. Then there was Felicani's vision and sheer stubbornness and, on occasion, when this failed, there was the faith and tolerance of his sons. For there were times, in periods of discouragement, when Felicani put it to his sons to throw the material away if they saw fit to do so. Somehow, when the flame guttered in the father, it still burned in Anteo and Arthur. Truly it can be said that it is the Felicani family who are our benefactors, and to whom we owe our thanks for this collection.

It must be understood that there were two Felicanis. I knew one well — the old, ill, tame, respected and respectable Felicani. But I caught glimpses, and he occasionally revealed to me, something of the earlier man, the European whose anarchism was not on the whole "philosophical." The Sacco-Vanzetti case was the beginning of the Americanization of Aldino Felicani. The people that this case brought him into contact with — Gardner Jackson, principally — drew Felicani out of one world and lodged him in another from which there was no return. I think it was from Jackson that Felicani learned about another kind of passion, another idealism, distinct from his own rough-and-tumble youthful anarchism, which I hasten to add, Felicani never completely abandoned. What Jackson showed Felicani concerned fundamental human decency and fair play in action.

During the meetings, in 1959, in support of Alexander Cella's petition to the Massachusetts legislature for a posthumous pardon for Sacco and Vanzetti, Felicani once spoke out to the absolute horror of the inner circle — old Professor Schlesinger among them — when he asked whether, if during the hearings the consensus seemed to be going against Sacco-Vanzetti, "Should we break the meeting up?" He said this with the old fire in his eye, and, using those wonderful hands of his, made a huge fist that spoke of a past in which he had been no stranger to violence and force.

Felicani was not a simple man — not as simple as he liked to give the impression. He could be quite cagey, and was never quick to reveal himself or give himself away. I had a great sense, for years, of his constant holding back. Not until the last few weeks of his life did he actually confide little-known or unknown things to me about Sacco and Vanzetti. He always confirmed my discoveries and intuitions — he never lied to me — but neither did he ever volunteer information. By the time I really got to know him it was too late; he was too old. Sacco and Vanzetti were enshrined, were too sacred. I think this was perhaps a limitation in Felicani, who was the one person in the position to have known both the private and the public side of the Sacco-Vanzetti case. Partisan always, he was unused to complete openness and frankness. But history must serve the Truth. Intellectually, Felicani knew this but emotionally he was too close to the cause of Sacco-Vanzetti to be able to act upon this. The men Sacco and Vanzetti had greatness. To my mind, they continue to stand out, undiminished by the passage of time, as the finest and purest product of the impact of the Italian on these shores. Truth cannot tarnish, but can only enhance them. Felicani himself was no mere cardboard figure; he too had his share of greatness. The collection that we present here tonight and that enriches us all, pays tribute to that greatness, pays tribute to his clear passion and singlemindedness. At the same time, it stands as a monument to the faith and to the hopes of Aldino Felicani.

Philip J. McNiff:

Thank you very much, Norman, for this very perceptive and illuminating account of one of the great figures in the 20th Century: Aldino Felicani, the man, who is one of the great collectors. His sense of preserving materials for the benefit of the future and his greatness is sharing this material for future generations is one of the great things of this period.

While we have heard about Aldino Felicani, the Man and his Collection, I think it is important also to have some personal reminiscences of this man who played such an important role in one of the landmark cases in Massachusetts and United States legal history. A person who also contributed a great deal to the social advancement of his country.

And now to speak in terms of personal reminiscences, we are very privileged to have a series of brief statements on Aldino Felicani, the man. I am pleased now first to present Oreste Fabrizi who will give his personal reminiscences.

Oreste Fabrizi:

I am glad to participate in this tribute to Aldino Felicani, but I must beg your forgiveness, for unlike those that preceded or will follow me, I will speak in Italian. This is my best tribute to our friend and comrade Felicani, for Italian is our mother tongue, that of Nicola Sacco and Bartolomeo Vanzetti for whose cause Aldino Felicani, using the same tongue, fought his most powerful, wonderful, and intense battles, first to try to snatch them from the hands of the executioners and later for the vindication of the crime which they had never committed and for which the court was tarnished with infamy for the cruel and preconceived sentence which has no equal in the system of justice of this country.

It will not be easy for me in such a short time and in so few unadorned words to say all that I would want to say about comrade Aldino. I had the luck and the pleasure of making his acquaintance back in 1927, and since that date we began to work united for the common cause until the day of his death.

Aldino Felicani was born in Vicchio, a small town in the province of Firenze in the year 1891. When he was 12 he moved with the family to Bologna where he began to work as an apprentice typographer.

There he met the two libertarian activists, Zavattero and Maria Rigier. The latter, imprisoned because of the usual accusation of offense to the press, offered Aldino the first occasion to continue publication of the anti-militarist paper *Rompete le File*, which exposed him to the risk of meeting the same end. But, continuously hounded by the police, he came to this country in 1914 and established his residence in Cleveland where he began publication of the magazine *La Questione Sociale*. Later he moved to New York where he did not mind working as a dishwasher first and later as a typographer. In 1918 he came to Boston where he worked as a linotypist for the newspaper *La Notizia* (the News); and later he bought a small printing shop, The Excelsior Press, where he worked with his two sons, Anteo and Arthur, until his death.

Due to him, the Committee for the Defense of Sacco and Vanzetti was formed, and he was its Treasurer. Immediately after, Aldino published *L'Agitazione* whose contents, translated into various languages, became known in many parts of the world. This was followed by *Controcurrent* and later by *Lantern*, written partly in English and partly in Italian, and later still by *Controcorrente,* which lasted until the fall of the Fascist regime, and then was suspended on various occasions but reappeared in 1957 and lasted to the end of its publisher's life.

I wish to underline now that Aldino wanted the first number which had the date July–August 1957 to be totally dedicated to remembering the legal assassination of the two martyrs.

Aldino Felicani, for his total dedication to the cause of Sacco and Vanzetti, is known all over the world. Unwavering adversary and anti-fascist fighter, he was an implacable enemy of any form of dictatorial regime. Since his adolescence and to the last breath of his life he was a very active participant whenever it was necessary to work for the defense of the oppressed and for human rights. A man of praiseworthy character, any time he wanted to reach his objective he became methodical, firm, and tenacious. In our innumerable conversations he would frequently remember the fights of the past, the good work accomplished, and that which should be accomplished in the future always with optimism, confidence, humility, and modesty. He was the crusader of every noble and just cause, and so he is remembered by all who knew him. For him it was always better to do a little than to do nothing — in the same style as that of the unforgettable Salvemini, who frequently repeated to us when we wanted to run at full speed, that if one disposes of only a thousand bricks it is not possible to build a palace where tens of thousands are needed.

A convinced defender of his ideal of human redemption, this idealistic anarchist from la Romagna, without pretense, without arrogance or insolence, always gave his work freely; and whenever the thermometer of *Controcorrente* reached a high fever, he asked me to remind the comrades and subscribers about our financial difficulties. Many bills of his printing press remained unpaid. His kindness and understanding was such that he did not have the strength to request what was owed to him, and he ventured to say to me: "Oreste, when they remember and have the money, they will come to see me." The door of the office of *Controcorrente,* which was the same door as that of the printing shop, was open equally to everybody. Aldino never asked from anyone his political identity. Because of his sensitivity for social, economic, and political problems he was loved and esteemed by many notable American liberals who on many occasions associated themselves with him. His presence inspired confidence in the success of any good cause, and this is the first reason why his friends multiplied and esteem for him increased progressively.

Controcorrente was an instrument of demolition, the arena where with measured precision he fought energetically and with passion against all the enemies of freedom, against violence and social injustice, and especially against Fascism that had in him one of its most obstinate adversaries. He was an intimate friend and a special admirer of Gaetano Salvemini who, from the pages of *Controcorrente* with exact, precise, and sharp documentation, refuted and destroyed the misdeeds of the Fascists, the Duce, and his praetorians.

Controcorrente was not the exclusive and personal newspaper of Aldino Felicani. Its pages were open to everybody. He wished that anyone that had something serious to say and document it would use it. From the most humble comrades there collaborated actively Nicola Tucci, Angelica Balabanoff, Massimo Salvadori, Giorgio Di Santillana, Davide Yona, Enzo Tagliacozzo, Gaetano Salvemini, and many others still, because they could write freely, refute the thoughts and actions of others without limitation or censorship. Aldino spent most of his time in the "Piccola Posta" which he retained as the most effective means of holding a direct dialogue with the comrades, of making his thinking better known and understood, of making known his thoughts and opinions, his reasons and the analysis of his liberal ideas.

He never spared his criticism of consuls, radio commentators, worthless journalists and all the petty colonial fights especially during the Fascist era. Relentless against all enemies of the proletariat, who were always unmasked on the pages of his magazine without pity and in an outspoken manner. Such was the style and design of the magazine that he never compromised his dignity or the dignity of the magazine both in criticism and protest.

As a member of the family of *Controcorrente* for a long time, giving my very modest part of work and cooperation, I can affirm tonight with pride and satisfaction that Aldino Felicani spent his entire life defending the humble and the oppressed. Never did he slacken or weaken in front of the enemy, never trade his ideals. Scrupulously conscious of his dignity, he was a man totally devoid of any personal interest, aiming only to the coming of a society more human, more responsible, fairer, where love, well being for all, peace, and human brotherhood would prevail. This is the man loved by comrades and friends and respected by enemies.

Tonight, his precious archives, so jealously cared for, on the tragic and cruel fate of the two innocent martyrs, are entrusted to the care of the Boston Public Library—and his most ardent desire is realized. Thus his mission ends, but there remains for us, and more appropriately for the young people, to find a way of honoring him and following his example and his teachings of human solidarity. His memory, solidly attached to the cause of Sacco and Vanzetti, will remain forever alive because it cannot be otherwise; because of the memory of the two martyrs that suffered the indelible act of injustice defined by Franklin Delano Roosevelt as the "most atrocious crime of human justice committed in this century."

Translated from the Italian by Benedetto Fabrizi, the speaker's son, and by Laura V. Monti, Keeper of Rare Books and Manuscripts, Boston Public Library.

Philip J. McNiff:

Thank you very much, Mr. Fabrizi, for this tribute to Aldino Felicani. For those of us who do not understand Italian fluently, this will be translated in the proceedings which will be published after the conference is over.

Now to read a translation of the tribute by Enzo Tagliacozzo, I wish to introduce Professor Marcello Garino, who came here from Italy as an interpreter for Miss Vanzetti who is with us this evening. It is now my privilege to present Professor Garino, who will read the tribute from Mr. Tagliacozzo.

Enzo Tagliacozzo:

More than 35 years have passed since I met Aldino Felicani in 1941 and yet my acquaintanceship and my frequent contacts with him between 1941–1944 form one of the most vivid experiences of my residence in the United States. The remembrance of him is intermingled with the three years in which I was near him, working at Harvard with Gaetano Salvemini as a research student. I went later for reason of work to New York, but I continued to send pieces for *Controcorrente* in the next two years. And with Salvemini, to whom Felicani was so attached, my friendship continued both in the United States and, when he returned, in Italy. It lasted until the day of his death in 1957.

Little more than 30, when I came to the United States after a period of one year in England, I got to know a milieu of anti-Fascists in America, already here for many years, and I found the means to attend Il Circolo Operaio di Somerville (the Workers' Circle of Somerville), I wonder if it still exists, where socialists and libertarians assembled in full fraternity of soul and interest even if the discussions which were held were often lively or actually raucous.

When, on the initiative of Salvemini and a group of his friends, The Mazzini Society began, the polemics became even more fierce. To these libertarians, the Mazzini Society seemed too moderate — some names among the directors were approved, others weren't — especially when it became interested

Translated from the Italian by Robert D'Attilio and Marcello Garino.

in allying itself with the clothing union led by Luigi Antonini, a friend of Roosevelt's and a friend, alas, of Generoso Pope's, too. Salvemini, and with him Felicani, did not have any admiration for Antonini; in their judgment he was too involved in unclear dealings with undesirable figures.

In Italy during the years of Fascism we were used to secret contacts among friends who were trusted anti-Fascists. Many of our best friends were in prison or in house arrest, for they had been too greatly involved in clandestine activity.

The Somerville club, the friends of Felicani, for me who came from a country by now deprived of liberty for many long years, gave the impression, almost physical, of that which must have been like the political workers' clubs of the pre-Fascist era, things which I knew from history books, not from personal experience. It was an atmosphere of brotherhood, even among men having different opinions and coming from different political experiences. I can remember a passionate invocation of the first of May spoken by Angelica Balabanoff with the enthusiasm and artistry of pre-Fascist Italy.

The heroic struggle Aldino Felicani fought to save his friends Sacco and Vanzetti from the electric chair is universally known. Those events always were part of his speeches. And later on he would have fought a tenacious battle to give light to Carlo Tresca's murder. But others have already spoken about the struggle for Sacco and Vanzetti and about "La Lanterna," and they know those times and events from personal experience.

I'll tell something about the man with whom I had frequent contacts between 1941 and 1944. I went to see him in his printing shop in the Italian quarter of Boston where he spent so many hours a day. The publication of *Controcorrente* must have cost him a lot every year, because the subscription covered only a small part of the expenses for printing it. Felicani was a printer, but he felt he had to use his savings to participate in the political campaigns which he felt to be his own. His son Anteo could testify to what we could only imagine because he never spoke about his financial difficulties. *Controcorrente* had to be published and was published with remarkable regularity and the collection of those years honors Felicani's efforts and memory.

In those years in Italy the word subversive had not a contemptible meaning. It only meant a man who, being afflicted with the injustices of the capitalistic society, wanted to transform it. I should say that during the Fascist period it was a title of honor to be indicated as a subversive by the police and by the Fascist press. Felicani came to America before the first World War because he was an antimilitarist and did not accept the draft. His old friends, those who are still alive, will certainly remember how Felicani lived in America during the first years after his arrival. I don't know if Felicani had to go through the experiences of so many Italian immigrants who were said to have slept on the floors of large crowded rooms and to have fed themselves with bananas during the first days after their arrival.

The impressive figure and the vigorous clasp of hands of this "good giant" hid a spirit of great sensibility that reacted promptly and instinctively against every injustice. And injustices involved America and the world. The violent society had had its issue in Fascism, in Nazism, and in Stalinism. Libertarian, anarchist in origin, Felicani had not certainly given up his deep convictions — that's to say that the best possible society would be the one substantiated by complete liberty and justice for everybody. But faced with the events of the twenty years between the two wars he had begun to soften his first positions. His absolute pacifism had begun to mitigate when he considered the necessity of preventing a Nazi victory in Europe and in the world. Though he did not cultivate any illusion about the internal regime of Soviet Russia, the human sacrifice of Russia in the war against the dictatorships of the right was undeniable and it had to be supported. That did not prevent him from reminding us that the Communist International had become, for many years, the *longa manus* of the Soviet Russian State and denouncing what the communists had done in Spain to smash the POUM, the anarchist opposition, Camillo Berneri's death, and many episodes which strengthened the profound aversion of a libertarian against Soviet Russian communism.

As for the United States, Felicani had learned to distinguish between the America of Harding and Hoover and that of Roosevelt. Between the two, as far as the cultural and political atmosphere was concerned, there was an abyss. Let's say it frankly, Felicani was not one of those men of the radical left who considered the Republicans and Democrats two different manifestations of capitalistic America. Perhaps

it was like this, but differences existed and they had to be recognized. And the social and pro-labor legislation of the New Deal was quite different from the blind conservatism of the Republicans and it had contributed to bringing the country out of the awful grasp of the world-wide economic crisis. And Roosevelt's foreign policy, after the errors and the hesitation of the first years, had first proposed America as the arsenal of democracy and then, with Lend Lease and intervention in the war, had contributed in a decisive way to the defeat of Nazi-Fascism. The Russian resistance itself, which was a major factor in the victory of the allied forces, would not have been possible without the war equipment provided by the America of Roosevelt. Felicani clearly saw and considered all this and he had a great admiration for Roosevelt's experienced ability.

Coming to the Italian side, I must say Felicani had a real great admiration for Salvemini whom he considered as an idol. The moral and intellectual esteem he had for the historian of Harvard exceeded that which he professed for any other anti-Fascist leader. The prodigious activity of this man during the American period stupefied him. And moreover he loved Salvemini's vehement character, his absolute moral intransigence, his disdainful refusal of any compromise with men and forces contrary to his ideals. Felicani not only appreciated all this, but he fully shared it.

And in my opinion, he would be pleased to know that, thanks to Ernesto Rossi, the collection of Salvemini's works, published by Feltrinelli, has almost been completed, which, incredible to say, has not yet happened for great figures of the Risorgimento like Mazzini, Catteneo, and Cavour.

In *Controcorrente* Felicani allowed Salvemini the space he wanted. And *Controcorrente* not only republished and translated Salvemini's articles which had appeared in American reviews, but Felicani, from time to time, succeeded in obtaining from Salvemini important original writings conceived for his monthly review which were directed to the Italians rather than to the Americans.

When Salvemini died, I sent Felicani some of the most meaningful contributions published to commemorate him in the Italian press. He put them together with other articles which appeared in American periodicals, and out of this emerged a critical survey evaluating Salvemini's political and historical work, copies of which, I hope, are still preserved.

In order to render the pages of *Controcorrente* more vivid and vital, he turned to some collaborators who were very close to Salvemini's way of evaluating the Italian and international situation. Among those collaborators we must remember Davide Jona, who month after month, while he lived, sent his comments. But during the years I spent in America, *Controcorrente* availed itself of the contributions, sometimes reprinted, sometimes original, of Giorgio De Santillana, Niccolo Tucci, Niccolo Chiaromonte, Lamberto Borghi, and many others including the author of these notes who between 1941 and 1944 collaborated assiduously with this Boston magazine. Certainly Salvemini and his friends in 1944 and 1945 were very busy with the bi-weekly *L'Italia Libera*; and then, after Mussolini's fall, Salvemini got in touch again with Ernesto Rossi and all the other numerous friends and admirers he had in Italy. And the faithful Felicani published, from time to time, the articles Salvemini wrote for *Il Ponte* of Calamandrei, *Critica Sociale* of Mondolfo, and others. But in 1944 to 1945 *L'Italia Libera* and *Controcorrente* supported each other. And in the issue which divided the Mazzini Society, Felicani and *Controcorrente* supported Salvemini's harsh criticism of Churchill's policy towards Italy, which wanted to save the monarchy, and Roosevelt's policy which — according to Salvemini — was to allow Churchill to do whatever he wanted in Italy. He also criticized the Sforza-Tarchiani and Ascoli group who didn't want to attack frontally the powerful leaders of Great Britain and United States.

I'll also point out the publication of a collection of pamphlets by *Controcorrente*: particularly valuable are Salvemini's writings "On the Relationship between State and Church" and "For a Republican and Socialist Concentration in Italy." It is almost superfluous to say that in the campaign for the abolition of Mussolini's Concordato with the Catholic Church, Felicani willingly supported Salvemini. And even nowadays that battle is far from won, because a Parliamentary majority for its abolition does not exist and because of the collaboration of the Communists with the Christian Democrats.

So, a lot of problems which were discussed and argued about on these pages, now made yellow by time, are still vital and up to date and moreover they count more for tomorrow than for the present. That's why I should ask Anteo Felicani, if he hasn't done it yet, to send a photocopy of *Controcorrente* to the Instituto Toscano per la Storia della Resistenza Italiana, which has its offices in Palazzo Medici Riccardi in Florence.

It would be the best way to preserve a part of Felicani's work and to help the studies on the years of the Second World War. When speaking of Felicani, my thoughts go to the friends that, like him, have left us: to Salvemini, the teacher of all of us; to Ernesto Rossi, his beloved disciple; to the Roselli brothers; to Santillana; Chiaromonte; Pannunzio; Jona; and others.

But it would be of some comfort to Felicani to know that Salvemini's thought is more alive than ever, that the volumes of his works have a large circulation in Italy, and that at least ten of his students are spreading his teaching through the Italian Universities. I can't close these short notes without remembering Felicani's great humanity and gentleness which were outstanding features of his family and of his friends too, and which brought him to participate in their difficulties, their joys, and their sorrows.

He provided all of us with the living image of what a better society would be; a society of men believing in the ideals of liberty and justice for everybody, men who are capable of translating their ideals into acts of everyday life.

Philip J. McNiff:

Thank you very much, Professor Garino, for reading the account of Mr. Tagliacozzo's tribute to Aldino Felicani. I am sure that Mr. Tagliacozzo's request to have material sent to Florence will be carried out. The next tribute will be by Anna Yona:

Anna Yona:

Mr. Felicani, as we used to call him, was the first Italian/American I met coming into the Boston area in the spring of 1942. My husband, my two children, and I came from New York to Cambridge where we were told to get in contact with Enzo Tagliacozzo, who at the time was assistant to Professor Salvemini.

We didn't know anyone, so we approached Mr. Tagliacozzo and went one evening to their apartment in Linnean Street in Cambridge. There I met Mr. Felicani. His towering figure, his typical anarchist attire, were the two things I first noticed. But when Enzo introduced him to me, it was his handshake that was the most salient attribute at that moment. We had come over to the United States from Italy, where it was not possible to express our feelings and opinions about the world's events. So, in meeting Felicani, my husband and I found a sense of fresh air, a feeling of freedom never felt before. I remember that first meeting. That first meeting was practically taken over by Salvemini; and all of us, including Felicani, were listening to Salvemini. But immediately we were attracted by the gentleness and at the same time by the boldness of Felicani's opinions and by the way he expressed them.

We started to visit him in his office, first in Blackstone Street; and then it was, when he was not busy, that I learned the tales and details in the Sacco-Vanzetti case. The fact is that in Italy the case had been exploited as a case against Fascism and therefore had been presented by the press in a completely biased way. Felicani, in all our meetings in his office, sometimes in the little eating place below the office, talked and described with passion the case, so that we became, my husband and I, very close friends. We cherished greatly the friendship that I feel he had for us. His way of talking was simple, but clear. Never nebulous or uncertain. His respect and trust for my husband's opinion was mutual and it never changed. He published a magazine *Counter Current*, and David and I had the privilege to write, especially my husband, in practically all the issues. Our lives really became alive after meeting him. Because in spite of his pessimism, he gave us a reason for living. To fight for equality and justice.

All during the War and after, we saw him practically at least once a week or we called each other as much. Our conversation was always about political events. During the McCarthy era, the Alger Hiss era, and the Tresca murder, there were endless discussions of what to do, how to react, how to fight against this reactionary movement. When in certain periods political events were not as pressing, the Sacco-Vanzetti case came out again and again. It had been, as it was his lifetime struggle, and he related to it most of the time, but not repetitiously. There was so much

to say that we didn't know. Every time we ended one of our meetings it was a new experience. He was also very affectionate towards my children, who were, I must admit, quite scared by his famous handshake because of its strength.

All during our long friendship we always called him Signor Felicani, while he called my husband and me by our first names. And as far as I remember he never asked us to call him in a different way. He was and is a legendary figure. For me and David he opened a new horizon to our minds and we were tremendously grateful for it. His passing left us with a void in our lives that could not be replaced.

Philip McNiff:

Thank you, Mrs. Yona. And now to conclude the personal tributes, Gardner Jackson, Jr.:

Gardner Jackson, Jr.:

Mr. McNiff, Anteo, Arthur, ladies and gentlemen. I was not yet four years old that summer night in August, 1927, when the good shoemaker and poor fish peddler were executed. And had not been born when the crime they were accused of committing occurred. Yet the case—the issues it raised and some of the lessons it taught—has been with me all of my life as a living thing.

At the earliest age of comprehension, I was aware that some tremendous event called Sacco and Vanzetti had taken place, but it was not until my father took me on a visit to Aldino's printing establishment — then on Hanover Street, I think—that the import of the tragic sequence of events commencing April 15, 1920 in South Braintree began to dawn on me. At the same time, it also began to dawn on me that between these two participants in that sequence, fashioned in a forge of ceaseless activity ending in seeming failure, was a bond that was something special.

After animatedly and fully responding to my fascination with the printing process (a fascination shared and approved of by my father, I think, who was always absorbed by any means of communication) by showing me how the various pieces of heavy machinery worked, the two settled down to the type of long rambling conversation with which I was to become familiar in the course of the other meetings between them I was fortunate enough to attend up until my father's death in 1965.

I cannot remember many of the specifics of what they talked about that day, nor many of the specifics of ensuing conversations. They always revolved about those facets of current social or economic activity and governmental response thereto, which they felt were unjust or oppressive. Taken as a whole, these conversations would be found, I think, to have comprised a litany of nearly every cause that moved socially minded men in the 20's, 30's, 40's and 50's: prejudice against minorities, the inroads of Fascism and Naziism, corporate anti-union activities and squeeze of the consumer, the sharecroppers and tenant farmers, the Spanish Civil War, the migrant worker, the Indian, the plight of the Blacks, they were all there.

Interesting as these specifics were, what came to impress me more was the relationship between the two and the strong chords and themes which began emerging as I listened. It is about these that I want to talk in memory of Aldino and, since my father is an integral part of my subject, I must talk about them both. I don't think Aldino would mind.

One is always fortunate, I think, to have the chance to observe social intercourse between people who are deeply fond of each other. This is simply because it is beautiful, and with beauty, it seems to me, one is dealing with essences in pursuit of which many admirable human quests are mounted. In the case of human relationship, the degree of beauty is correlated to the desire and capacity of the participants to communicate their pleasure in each other through expressional bonds of interest and concern; understanding, respect and appreciation; projection and anticipation; trust, faith, joy, zest and stimulation. The desire and capacity of Aldino and my father always seemed to me limitless.

I can recall, after we moved to Washington, D.C., accompanying my father one day to Union Station to meet Aldino. I always loved going to that vastly vaulted, echoing place, with its mixture of scurrying and almost inanimate people and its rumbling, hissing, somewhat terrifying monsters bringing floods of people from all of those places I wanted to visit. It was an arena, for me, of mystery and romance. I was absorbed with these fascinations when Aldino's train came in. As was his wont, my father set out vigorously down the platform with me trotting to keep up with him. And then there was Aldino's tall, large, flowing figure coming towards us. My father's pace quickened as did Aldino's, joy expressed in both their faces. They embraced and then, looking at each other, began concerned inquiry as to the state of mind and well being of the other. The little boy's fascination with the station receded as the warmth of their feelings overflowed to him.

I can also remember a number of dinners in Boston, in later years, at the Athens Olympia — it was always the Athens Olympia — often also attended by Arthur Schlesinger, Sr. I can see Aldino, wearing his ever present string tie, gesticulating gracefully with his long expressive hands to emphasize some gently stated point or thesis. I can feel the import of the matters discussed, but also the curiosity, humor, gaiety and zest with which and from which both purely gave and got pleasure. I can hear Aldino calling my father "Gardner" — he was the only one I ever knew who did so, he was "Pat" to everybody else — when he wanted to underscore a point or inquiry, and I can hear my father starting his response, "Now Aldino...", both looking intently at each other the while. Fond memories.

And as to the chords — and here I hasten to say that I do not presume to speak for either Aldino or my father, but rather I am stating the themes and values which seemed to me to underlie their conversation — they (the chords) emerged not from men embittered by the seeming failure represented by the executions nor from the sharp, self-righteous attacks which characterize the conduct of some causists; rather they emerged from the gentle, wondering, troubled, but consistent, carefully thought out and actively articulated resistance to what they considered inhuman in conduct and processes at all and varying levels of human activity, of two men, who, while reverential towards the pain and suffering occasioned by the Sacco and Vanzetti tragedy, and indeed, toward the element of tragedy underlying all life, were impelled by a joyful interest in and zest for it to make their contribution to its processes.

The chord that seemed to sound most frequently was struck with the words "the individual" and "relationships." Most points of departure seemed to revolve about concern over these. In the course of repeated reference, these views of life and human affairs emerged:

That given the gift of consciousness and with it an awareness of mortality's frailties, a person's sense of well being (sense of individuality or identity) is correlated to the degree to which he or she, through development and use of his or her capabilities, is able to relate and contribute to others and his or her environment and that the satisfaction of these experiences is, in turn, correlated to the well being of the latter (latter being others and the environment).

That the term "individuality" itself connotes relationships with other humans and the environment, the aggregate of which constitute society, and indeed, is meaningless without them, operating in accordance with what I have come to term the "individuality–relationship" equation which says that the more a person develops and uses his or her capabilities, the more individual he or she is and the more he or she has with which to relate and that the more he or she relates, the more individualized he or she becomes.

That the degree of relationship experienced is correlated to understanding of and reverence for the wonder of creation's system of relationships and the degree to which the individual is able to integrate the flow of his or her life with its transcendental flows.

That attempts to control, rather than guide individuals, organizations, the course of events or the environment tend to destroy relationships with these, first by the implied reduction in viability that the assumption of the possibility of control connotes, and ultimately by inevitable failure and rejection.

That a major aim of all socio-economic and governmental processes should be to assure all a chance to achieve an adequate livelihood without which consideration of individuality or individual rights becomes a futile exercise.

That since a person's work, as a source of livelihood and conduit for and shaper of relationships with others and the environment, is often a prime source of identity, and since a person's productivity is related to the identity he or she derives from work, all employers' policies should, within the context of collective aim and incorporating humor's balm, be directed toward assuaging that enemy of individuality and relationship, concern for one's security with its underlying emotions of guilt and fear of failure and/or rejection, and toward nurturing their handmaidens, full development and use of capabilities, exercise of curiosity, and exploration of hope's horizons.

That these policies and, in the long run, organizational aims will be enhanced by organizational concern for, and contribution to, society and environment.

That a prerequisite to the expression of individuality and its relationships is a free society in which expression itself, through thought or action, is unfettered by legal or psychological constraints other than those governing malicious harm to others or environment.

Parenthetically, it was the central interest in the individual which, I think, led my father to write for the March 1929 issue of *The Lantern*, which Aldino and he edited, in response to the contention that President Lowell was just a representative of a system that demanded the execution of Sacco and Vanzetti:

We are not interested in systems. We are interested in individual human character. We believe that the characters in the dominant positions in society determine the quality of that society. We believe that systems are secondary.

And again, parenthetically, their judgement of character was endorsed by Walter Lippmann, who wrote for the August 1929 memorial issue of *The Lantern:*

If Sacco and Vanzetti were professional bandits, then historians and biographers who attempt to deduce character from personal documents might as well shut up shop. By every test that I know of for judging character, these are the letters [the letters of Sacco and Vanzetti] of innocent men…

A corollary theme to which there was constant reference was the corrupting influence of power and supporting hero cultisms. Drives for its achievement were seen as involving human manipulation through stimulation of the various prejudices and fears to which humans are subject, and the responses to play upon these were clearly identified as sad impediments to human development. As I listened, I found that threaded through the discourse was a sense of the destructive effects that the thrust for control can have upon relationship and of its futility as a brake upon time and mortality.

Embedded in their discussions of power was a constant suspicion of competition. Here I find my only disagreement with their philosophy and even this is simply in terms of the degree to which they seemed to write off competition as a useful human tool. There is no question as to numerous acts and flows antithetical to human development perpetrated under cover of worship at competition's altar. And there is a certain illogic in its deification by those whose daily preoccupation is seeking to eliminate it through exercise of personal power and/or economic combination. However, when engaged in within the context of genuine relationship, it seems to me to serve mankind in energizing the pursuit of excellence, in demarking its attainment, and in encouraging tensions without which life can be dilatory and shapeless. It is, of course, one of the engines of evolution.

Opponents have categorized them as typical, hand-wringing do-gooders who would destroy the moral fabric of society and undermine its economic viability with the principles and programs they espoused. Yet I can think of none who were more insistent upon the urgency of each individual's responsibility to self and society to earn his or her living, to respect and engage energetically in common affairs, and to maximize his or her contribution to both through continuing expansion of his or her base of knowledge, sensitivity and intellectual abilities.

They differed from many of their critics, I think, in having an optimistic view of human nature and its potential which held that if given opportunity and encouragement, individuals will reach out toward potential, rather than accept without giving of themselves, subsiding into non-contributory dependence. Their quarrel was with all governmental, economic and societal systems which seemed to them to deny or restrict the individual's quest for identity and fulfillment through policies and actions emanating, at best, from acceptance and use of the motivational forces of fear and greed, and, at worst, from transforming surrender to them from sin to virtue. They saw a world society with the means and technology to provide enough for all which, primarily because of these motivations, did not and thus limited the potential for transcendental experience. For, you see, they, like John Donne, believed that the ultimate sin was separateness and with him knew "for whom the bell tolls."

And though they were most concerned with where accelerating cultural evolution was leading, and with immediate means of changing the seeming direction in which the rapid successive bursts of the agricultural, industrial and technological revolutions were thrusting us, there was sufficient reverence to substantiate in them the wonder at the interrelationship of all things within the matrix of space and time — that convergence of which Professor Wilson speaks — which moved Vanzetti to write from his cell upon receipt of a postcard depicting Niagara Falls of its bringing him "…a glance of the immense awe of Nature, and an echo of its idiom into my soul…."

It is thus not surprising that they should select for emphasis those reciprocally enhancing human inclinations and capabilities — those of thought, cooperation and sharing — which were essential to the evolutionary success of those social animals who descended from the trees some twelve million years ago, our hominid ancestors, and those inclinations and capabilities in the exercise and expansion of which lie concurrently the greatest pleasures in life and the best hope for survival of *homo sapiens*.

I never heard either of them speak of Teilhard de Chardin but cannot help but feel that they would have been deeply interested in his conclusions as to a latent consciousness in all matter and the emergence, as a natural consequence of evolution, of a layer of life above the biosphere which he called the noosphere, the sphere of consciousness.

These then are the memories and thoughts which pass through my mind in recollection of the happy association of these two spirits. Though they failed in the immediate ends of the cause that brought them together and in a number of others in which they joined hands, time and the transcendence of the values they espouse have turned as they so often do, many defeats into triumphs. If momentarily defeated, they were never vanquished, nor indeed were Sacco and Vanzetti. If the shadows they cast are not formidable, they are enheartening and make me very glad that through my father, Aldino came my way.

Philip J. McNiff:

Thank you very much, Mr. Jackson. Through these several personal tributes to Aldino Felicani, we've learned something of his expertise in collecting and preserving a facet of history which is important to the understanding of contemporary civilization. We have learned of the integrity and the humanity of this man, Aldino.

And now we are going to have Mr. Cella give a commentary on the description of the funeral procession of Sacco and Vanzetti, which was put together by Aldino Felicani.

Mr. Cella has been actively involved in the Sacco and Vanzetti case for a good many years. He played an important role in the program which was put on at the State House.

Alexander Cella:

Thank you very much, Mr. McNiff, Miss Vanzetti, Arthur, Anteo. It is my great privilege and honor this evening to be able to read to you, in conjunction with the film which we are now going to see, the description of the funeral procession of Sacco and Vanzetti in the words of Aldino himself.

"In the meantime I had ordered thousands of red armbands with black words on them 'Justice Crucified —August 22–23, 1927.' Then Sunday morning came. It was a very gloomy day, almost raining. I started to see people that I knew. I saw people from Chicago, from Detroit, from Paterson, New Jersey, from New York. There was a tremendous influx of people from everywhere. It was an incredible thing. It was hard to walk through Hanover Street. The side streets were just crowded with people. It was just a mass of human beings. We were at the headquarters and we were distributing the armbands. Joe Moro and all the others were around. We decided to start the procession from the North End Park. I told them to put the armbands on three or four blocks from the North End Park. I was in the car with Rosa Sacco and Luigia Vanzetti. It was the family car following the hearse. We started around one o'clock, in the early afternoon. I wish I had the power of describing the mass of people concentrated in that part of town.

The North End Park was a large park and it was full of people, as well as Hanover Street. They were

on the roofs and the windows. I wondered why those houses didn't fall down. When the armbands were put on, the police and the horses started into action. There were so many people, they couldn't move. Tributes of flowers came from everywhere. There were cars and cars and cars of flowers. Beautiful flowers. There were many flowers in the headquarters.

When we reached Scollay Square, there was a newsstand distributing *The Nation*. *The Nation* had one cartoon on the front page by Boardman Robinson. "Justice Crucified," something to that effect. Distribution of *The Nation* started there. That was when the police attacked. Jumping on the people with horses and breaking the line of the funeral.

When we reached Tremont Street there was a break in the line. It started to rain pretty hard. The people were walking without coats and hats. It was impossible to go down Beacon Street. It was impossible to use other streets. But we finally reached the place where the bodies were cremated.

The violence of the police at Forest Hill was something I can't describe. The people were clubbed and were almost killed. The bodies were cremated at Forest Hill. There was a mob of people from Beacon to Forest Hill. The newspapers that evening talked about millions of people watching and watching, with the rain coming down in buckets. We reached Forest Hill and Jackson had written the farewell address. We decided that Mary Donovan should read it. They wanted me to do it. I was not up to anything of that sort. Mary Donovan was very glad to do it and she did it well. The chamber in the cemetery was very small; an ordinary chamber in a crematorium. It was a very moving business really. After that was over, people just went back to the city. I went that night to accompany Mrs. Sacco and Mrs. Vanzetti to where they were living. I spent some time with them, then I went home. That was all."

Philip J. McNiff:

Thank you very much, Al, for that very moving reading accompanying the film.

Now it is my pleasure to present a friend of Aldino Felicani and the Felicani family. A person who has been actively involved in a wide variety of library activities over the years. A man who has served with distinction on the City Council and a Representative to the General Court. A person who is in no small measure responsible for the advance of libraries and the development of resources in libraries in the Commonwealth of Massachusetts, Mr. Gabriel Piemonte:

Gabriel Piemonte:

Miss Vanzetti, Anteo, Arthur, Director McNiff and friends.

For me it was a privilege to have had my life enriched with the experience of knowing Aldino Felicani. No only knowing him, but actually being a beneficiary of Felicani the man, a beneficiary in a material way because of his public life and his ability in getting across his message. Much has been said; much more could be said about Aldino Felicani. But I am reminded of the visit to this country just a few days ago of His Holiness the Pope. I was reminded of the words proclaimed when addressing the United Nations Assembly. And if ever there were an observation that really and truly summed up the philosophy of Felicani it was these words: "Each man and woman is endowed with dignity as a human person, with his or her own culture, experiences and aspirations, tensions and sufferings and legitimate expectations." Isn't that a really true description of Aldino Felicani? Of course it is.

How fortunate we are — how fortunate I am, to have continued in the line of service, of being privileged to continue my association with the Felicani boys. Seeing Anteo and Arthur, it has been a privilege to serve them, and in serving them, to know them. If anyone was a chip off the old block, each of them is. Each of them is endowed with the characteristics that were Aldino's. Too often in life we forget the one big thing that is necessary in life. Hope. Hope. Hope. Isn't that what Aldino was expressing? Isn't that what he was giving out? Yes, Sacco and Vanzetti was a great moral event, but doesn't it also portray the fact that Aldino was doing then just what his boys are doing today when they unselfishly give the world for all times the benefit of these papers? And aren't we fortunate that it happened at a time when the city has as its library director a man who himself, Director McNiff, has given so much and who cares. With this thought I would like to have you share with me the pleasure of hearing Anteo and Arthur Feli-

cani. And now I present to you Anteo and Arthur Felicani.

Anteo Felicani:

Thank you, Mr. Piemonte, Mr. McNiff, ladies and gentlemen. This is a momentous occasion and we are very happy to be here. It seems to me that when a great event comes to a successful conclusion, that it is not difficult to find many who would share in the fruits of victory and few who would take the responsibility of defeat. Unfortunately for us, most of the principals concerned with these papers have passed away and all too many of them have been unheralded and unrecognized for their important contributions and dedication to this cause.

With this thought in mind, we would like to draw your attention to a man who, I think, was probably the most important of these people. He was a long-time associate and fellow worker with my father and, strangely enough, my brother and me. His name was Manlio Reffi. Known to all simply as "Reffi" or "Mr. Reffi."

Mr. Reffi was the son of a stone cutter from San Marino who settled in Barre, Vermont. He was a tall, erect man, well over six feet. He had a fair complexion, a wide face and very large, expressive eyes. At an early age Mr. Reffi chose to be a printer and, after working in Connecticut and Rhode Island, came to Boston and worked side by side with my father. They were both linotype operators. These two men soon became fast friends and were the ones who produced the first Sacco-Vanzetti Defense Committee journals. As a matter of fact, Reffi's name appeared on the first papers produced. Mr. Reffi was a proud man, proud of his family and his San Marino background. He was also a generous person who was always ready to help and give that extra effort to anyone who needed assistance. He was a quiet and unassuming person and had a great sense of morality.

Mr. Reffi believed very strongly that it was impossible to compromise a principle because, he realized, once allowed, the principle no longer existed.

I can remember how incensed he became when some people killed a story in a publication which we were printing because it offended a very rich and influential person. He wasn't the only one who was incensed; the editor quit. We realize that this is not the tribute that Mr. Reffi deserves but simply an acknowledgement that we are aware of the great contributions and sacrifices that he made to this collection and that we have not forgotten him.

Many people have said to us that if this collection is so important and valuable, how come you don't sell it? It is a fair question, but it shows an unawareness of the contents of these papers. These papers cannot belong to anyone — they belong to everyone. The very character and nature of this collection makes it impossible to put a price on them — even in this money-oriented society. After witnessing the struggles, the defeats, the honesty and unselfishness of those who were dedicated to this cause, it would be a betrayal to their memories to consider accepting any money whatsoever. We have to remember two men gave their lives for it; my father and his friends devoted a lifetime to it.

These papers were not meant to be in the hands of any self-serving individuals or in any private institution. They belong to all of humanity.

We are very happy and proud to have this collection here in this great institution, the Boston Public Library. Over the main entrance of this library is the declaration: "Free to All" — which means to us free to the rich and poor alike; to the sick and infirm; free to the strong; free to the blacks, the whites and to all of the other peoples of the world; free to the religious and non-religious; free to everyone.

If these papers bring a keener insight to help solve the seemingly never ending battle against man's inhumanity to his fellow man — the struggles, the sacrifices and the dedication of all those persons who made this collection possible would agree that it was well worth it. Thank you.

Philip J. McNiff:

Thank you very much, Anteo. Your very moving statement not only is in reference to the Felicani collection, but to what libraries and civilization are all about. This is what this institution intends to do — make these papers available to all scholars, to all people, who can preferably utilize these in terms of making advances for humanity, for human understanding, for integrity, the things which your father and his associates stood for.

We are honored and pleased to be the recipient of these papers. This institution, which is one of the great research public institutions in this country and in the world, will maintain these papers, will service them and make them available for future generations of people, with a keen understanding that they represent the best of what your father had hoped for. We are privileged on this very significant occasion to have with us Ms. Vincenzina Vanzetti, sister of Mr. Vanzetti, and I am pleased now to introduce her to this audience. She has a few words to say which will be translated by her friend Professor Garino.

Vincenzina Vanzetti

First of all I'd like to thank Mr. McNiff and his assistants and staff for the invitation they have kindly sent me.

I must confess I had thought never to come to the United States of America for understandable reasons. What we had suffered in all these 50 years prevented me from considering a travel to the United States as a thing I could do.

But reading my brother's letters over and over again I discovered that America was not only the country in which he had ended his life in so a tragical way, but also a country in which so many people had shared its tragedy and helped him as much as they could. Moreover my sister Luigina who came to the United States a few days before his death had told me about the atmosphere of friendship and fraternity she had found here. So I began to distinguish between the institutions of the time who had wanted the trial and the death sentence and the people, those marvellous people who felt Sacco and Vanzetti's tragedy as their own.

The visits I had in Italy from many American scholars and researchers, the books they published, the way they treated the case, convinced me that a visit of mine could mean something even for them. Lastly came the invitation of the Boston Public Library and I told our friend Robert D'Attilio I accepted, though I am age 76.

When landing in Boston airport I thought about the way my brother Bartolomeo had come to the United States. What a nice difference. Boston itself has changed since the first years of this century. But when I first met the people who had invited me, I felt at home and I realized that Bartolomeo could have felt the same with the Felicani and Brini family, just to remember some of those he loved best.

I really must thank Anteo and Arthur Felicani for the donation of their collection to the Library. I hope scholars, historians and especially the younger generation will find in it new sources to understand history and how a perverse public power can destroy lives of men when they have different opinions and firmly act according to their ideals. What I hope is to know the truth. Sacco and Vanzetti are already rehabilitated in the conscience of millions of men all over the world but the case is not closed. I am sure this conference will help to draw new attention to the study of the case, to the social background of the time, to the behavior of Sacco and Vanzetti as anarchists and as men whose concern was a better society. I am not a historian, I feel the truth in my heart but I think people must know what happened and why, because history can teach future generations. No man must be sentenced to death because of his ideas and political behavior. I am sure your work will help to reach this purpose.

Philip J. McNiff:

Thank you very much, Miss Vanzetti. You have honored us by accepting the invitation to be with us here for this conference.

We now have a reception upstairs and a chance to see the exhibition which has been put together for the occasion. I also wish to express appreciation to my late associate Francis Moloney who had worked assiduously with Mr. D'Attilio in putting this conference together. His tragic death was a serious blow to all of us and the proceedings which we will publish will be done in his memory as well as in memory of Aldino Felicani and the cause which we celebrate in this conference.

Illustrations

1

2

3

1. Ferdinando Sacco, shortly after his arrival
   in America, *circa* 1908.

2. Bartolomeo Vanzetti, photographed with
   beard, during the period of his trip to
   Mexico, 1917–18.

3. Photograph of Sacco and Vanzetti taken
   during their trial; the basis of Ben Shahn's
   well-known work.

40786 - Felicani Aldino di Torquato

4

5

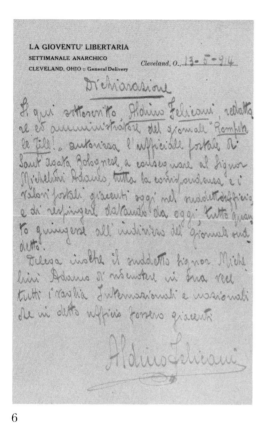

6

7

4. The arrest photograph of Aldino Felicani, taken for his anti-war activities in Italy, 1912. *Archivio Centrale dello Stato, Rome.*

5. Aldino Felicani and others during an anarchist picnic in Philadelphia, summer of 1915. *Hugo Rolland Archives, International Institute of Social Studies, Amsterdam. Courtesy of Mrs. Siphra Rolland.*

6. Felicani's attempt to recover money and correspondence from his suppressed journal, *Rompete Le File (Break Ranks)*, in Bologna. It is written on the letterhead of his new journal, *La Gioventú Libertaria (Libertarian Youth)*, published in Cleveland.

7. *L'Agitazione,* the Sacco-Vanzetti Defense Committee journal, edited by Aldino Felicani. An issue shortly after the conviction of the two men, August 20, 1921.

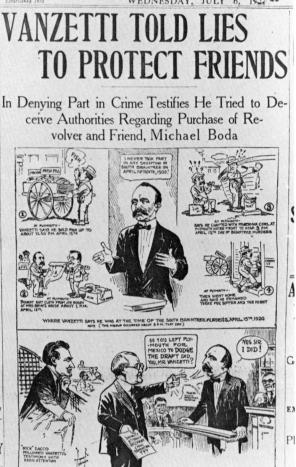

8

8. Cartoons by Norman, drawn for the *Boston Post* during the Sacco-Vanzetti trial. *Newspaper collection, Boston Public Library.*

9. The arrest photograph of Luigi Galleani, editor of *Cronaca Sovversiva*, taken in Italy after his deportation from America in 1919. *Archivio Centrale dello Stato, Rome.*

10. *Cronaca Sovversiva*, the newspaper edited by Luigi Galleani and supported by Sacco and Vanzetti.

9

10

Leggete

LA SALUTE
E' IN VOI

25 cents

Sebastiano Faure.

Dio non esiste!
DODICI PROVE DELLA INESISTENZA DI DIO

Traduzione di
ANTONIO CAVALAZZI

10c
OGNI COPIA

11

LA SALUTE É IN VOI

Si distribuisce gratis

12

ANNO I — No. 1   BOSTON, MASSACHUSETTS   GIUGNO 1926

PROTESTA UMANA
Bollettino del Comitato di difesa Sacco e Vanzetti
74 Indirizzo: SACCO-VANZETTI DEFENSE COMMITTEE, P. O. Box 93 Hanover Street Station, Boston, Mass.

Mentre s'approssima il giorno dell'esecuzione i reclusi ammoniscono: LA SALUTE E' IN VOI!

L'infamia suprema

Nell'ultimo periodo di questi sei lunghi anni di lotte per salvare dall'infamia della pena capitale Sacco e Vanzetti, v'è stato un tempo in cui tutti carez-

cosa a quelli che detengono i pubblici poteri.

Di qua è la massa inerme, diversa per razza, lingua e costume, che, in una mirabile fusione di spiriti, con unica voce chiede · giustizia — un nuovo proceso per i reclusi innocenti.

minciò, fra la ostilità, il pregiudizio, l'isteria dei puritani, Si compie come un linciaggio sadica d'una plebaglia satura di fanatismo e d'orgoglio.

Se fossimo stati meno cristiani e meno fiduciosi nella giusti-

Il Nuovo Processo Negato

[WATERBURY REPUBLICAN]

Dispiace molto che la Corte Suprema del Massachusetts abbia negato un nuovo processo a Nicola Sacco e Bartolomeo Vanzetti. Per quanto possa essere giudicato legalmente corretto il processo dei due italiani, vi sono dei fatti non

dei buoni cittadini della Conteo Norfolk, Mass., all'epoca del delitto e del processo; in quel periodo di tempo che seguiva immediatamente l'isterismo rosso che invase il paese dopo la guerra e risultò nella "Crociata Rossa". Il sentimento pubblico contro gli stranieri era ancora violento. Ciò risultò dal processo, quando il magistrato dell'accusa cercò di eccitare il pregiudizio contro

calma e più sana. In breve, gli accusati furono con tutta probabilità condannati come radicali stranieri e renitenti alla coscrizione militare anzichè come assassini.

Tutto ciò fu così ovvio che l'organizzazione radicali in tutto il mondo fecero loro il caso e ciò ha aumentato non poco il pregiudizio degli stranieri contro questo paese. Ciò può essere facil-

13

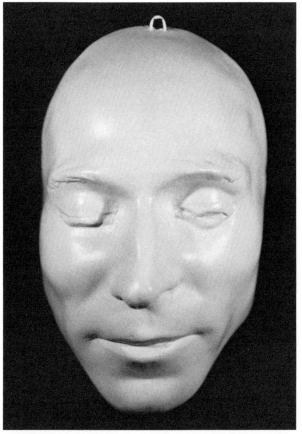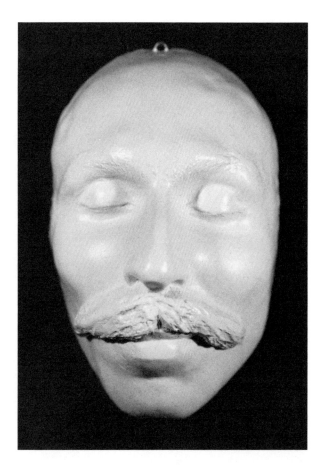

14

11. Anarchist pamphlet, translated from the French of Sebastien Faure by Antonio Cavalazzi, an editor of *Cronaca Sovversiva*. Printed in Lynn, Massachusetts, in 1915. The pamphlet contains a notice for *La Salute è in Voi* on the back cover.

12. *La Salute è in Voi (Health Is Within You)*, an Italian language bomb manual, probably written in Europe, but distributed in the United States.

13. *Protesta Umana (The Human Protest)*, journal of the Sacco-Vanzetti Defense Committee, printed shortly after the rejection of legal appeals by the Massachusetts Supreme Court, with a front page statement signed by Sacco and Vanzetti.

14. The death masks of Sacco and Vanzetti. Six original pairs exist; one is now in the Boston Public Library. *Photographs by Paul Petricone.*

15

WHAT I WISH MORE THAN ALL IN THIS
LAST HOUR OF AGONY IS THAT OUR
CASE AND OUR
FATE   MAY BE UNDERSTOOD
IN THEIR   REAL BEING AND SERVE
AS A   TREMENDOUS LESSON TO
THE   FORCES OF   FREEDOM
SO THAT OUR SUFFERING AND DEATH
WILL NOT HAVE BEEN IN VAIN

16

15. Funeral procession of Sacco and Vanzetti
    passing through Scollay Square, Boston,
    August 28, 1927.

16. Model in plaster for memorial bas-relief
    of Sacco and Vanzetti by noted sculptor
    Gutzon Borglum, now on permanent dis-
    play in the Boston Public Library.

17

18

17. Photograph during the conference held
    on the occasion of the presentation of the
    Felicani collection to the Boston Public
    Library, October, 1979. From left to right:
    Anteo and Arthur Felicani, sons of Aldino
    Felicani; Vincenzina Vanzetti, sister of
    Bartolomeo Vanzetti; Marcello Garino,
    friend and translator of Miss Vanzetti;
    Caterina Caldera, Miss Vanzetti's cousin;
    and Gabriel Piemonte, friend of the Feli-
    cani family.

18. Anteo Felicani talking with Library Direc-
    tor Philip J. McNiff on the occasion of the
    presentation of the Felicani papers to the
    Boston Public Library.

Sacco-Vanzetti: The Anarchist Connection

Introductory Remarks

Nunzio Pernicone
University of Illinois

This morning we will address ourselves to the anarchist dimension of the case. Regrettably, if you were to examine the six or seven major works on the case (on exhibit outside), you would find, with almost no exception, practically nothing contained in those books about the Italian anarchist movement in the United States; that is to say, the social, political, intellectual and spiritual ambience in which Sacco and Vanzetti lived, fought, and ultimately died. It still remains a veritable unknown and uncharted world. Unfortunately, I think part of the neglect is due to overt political prejudice of one sort or another. We know Sacco and Vanzetti were anarchists. Nevertheless, the word "anarchist" still connotes the image of a swarthy, hirsute, demonic looking creature with a bomb in one hand and a knife between his teeth, ready to do violence to society at large. There were a few anarchists like that, but for the most part that is, of course, an absurd stereotype.

Paradoxically, among people who believed Sacco and Vanzetti were guilty and fairly tried, and people who believed they were innocent and grossly railroaded, you will find certain similarities in their approach to this question, especially in terms of their distorting the anarchist ideals of these men and in ignoring the movement to which they belonged. Judge Webster Thayer—you will recall the charming phrase he used—said that the ideas of the defendants were "cognate with crime," and that to be an anarchist is *ipso facto* to be a criminal. Others of conservative persuasion—the historian Robert Montgomery, for example—assume that to be true and proceeded accordingly. Naturally Sacco and Vanzetti were guilty: they were anarchists. However, if you look at the other end of the political spectrum, many liberal historians who have studied the case, while arguing vehemently that these men were innocent and unfairly tried, are disturbed—almost embarrassed—by the fact that Sacco and Vanzetti were anarchists. They don't know what to do with this problem. Consequently, they call them "philosophical anarchists," a term in the liberal lexicon which is a euphemism for harmless utopians whom nobody need take seriously. What our speakers today will prove beyond any doubt is that these men were not philosophical anarchists; they were genuine, militant revolutionaries. Whether you agree with their position or not is beside the point. These were men who believed that, in order to transform society, to realize liberty and justice, capitalist society, as it existed in their time, had to be overthrown, and overthrown violently. Accordingly, our three speakers will approach them as revolutionaries. We will have the larger dimensions of the Italian anarchist movement sketched in by Professor Paul Avrich, Professor of History at Queens College of the City University of New York. Professor Avrich is the dean of anarchist studies in this country. I don't know of anyone who has studied so many different aspects of anarchist history and anarchist ideas; he has published innumerable books on the subject, his most recent, a beautiful little portrait of the woman anarchist Voltairine de Cleyre. Professor Avrich today will speak about the Italian anarchist movement in the United States. I give you our first speaker.

Paul Avrich, Queens College, City University of New York

Italian Anarchism in America: An Historical Background to the Sacco-Vanzetti Case

A few years ago I received a phone call from a woman in New York City who told me that she was planning to write a book about Sacco and Vanzetti. She wanted to know what sources there were about their lives and activities. I asked her if she read Italian: I was going to recommend *La Cronaca Sovversiva* and other Italian anarchist journals. She said, "No, I don't." "In that case," I said, "I think you ought to abandon the project, unless you are prepared to learn the language well enough to read it." She replied that she was not interested in the anarchist aspect of the case. I told her that it was essential for her to study the anarchist movement if she planned to do any serious work on Sacco and Vanzetti, to which she replied: "The anarchists are not serious people, and I prefer not to deal with that aspect of the case." At this point, I strongly urged her to embark on some other subject that was more congenial to her interests.

For one cannot deal with Sacco and Vanzetti without talking about anarchism; and, as Professor Pernicone pointed out, the greatest single shortcoming in the literature on the case—a literature that is vast, enormous—is its failure to come to grips with Sacco and Vanzetti as anarchists. Anarchism was a central feature of their lives. To write about Sacco and Vanzetti without talking about the anarchist connection, the anarchist dimension, is equivalent to writing about Eugene Victor Debs without talking about socialism, or to writing about Lenin and Trotsky without talking about communism. Anarchism was the passion, the great idea of Sacco and Vanzetti. It was the driving force of their lives. It was their obsession, their love, their chief interest on a day-to-day basis.

I'd like to read three quotations from their writings which illustrate this point. First, a quotation from Vanzetti's brief autobiography, *The Story of a Proletarian Life:*

> I am and will be until the last instant (unless I should discover that I am in error) an anarchist-communist, because I believe that communism is the most humane form of social contract, because I know that only with liberty can man rise, become noble, and complete.

We find a similar idea in Sacco's writings—for example, in one of his last letters to his son Dante, written on August 18, 1927, five days before the execution. He advises Dante to help the persecuted and oppressed "as your father and Bartolo fought and fell yesterday for the conquest of the joy of freedom for all and the poor workers." One final quotation—we can find numerous statements of this kind in their manuscripts and published works — from a letter of Vanzetti to Virginia MacMechan, who was one of those Boston "Brahmins" of whom Professor Solomon spoke so eloquently yesterday, who helped to teach him English in prison. This letter dates from 1923, right in the middle of the case:

> Oh friend, the anarchism is as beauty as a woman for me, perhaps even more, since it include all the rest and me and her. Calm, serene, honest, natural, vivid, muddy and celestial at once, austere, heroic, fearless, fatal, generous and implacable—all these and more it is.

Sacco and Vanzetti, then, were two of the many thousands of Italian anarchists in the United States. What I'd like to do for the remaining 15 or 20 minutes

61

of my talk is to give you some general idea of what the Italian anarchist movement was like, the movement to which these two men dedicated their energies and ultimately their lives: its origins, its ideas, its chief figures, its activities. This is a very difficult thing to do in such a brief period of time, but in the afternoon session, when we discuss the case in greater detail, if anybody has specific questions about this or that aspect of the Italian anarchist movement, I and the other participants will be happy to try to answer them.

The first Italian anarchist groups in the United States appeared in the 1880s, at the same time as the beginnings of large-scale Italian immigration into this country. Most of these immigrants were of the peasant and working classes, and the anarchists came largely from these segments of Italian society. The initial group was formed in 1885 in New York City, which became a leading center of Italian anarchism in America. It was called the Gruppo Anarchico Rivoluzionario Carlo Cafiero, Cafiero being one of the most famous of the anarchist leaders in Italy in the late nineteenth century. Another group of the same name was formed two years later in Chicago, the most important center of Italian anarchism in the midwest. The first newspaper published by the Italian anarchists in the United States appeared in 1888. It was called simply *L'Anarchico*, The Anarchist, and was issued by the Cafiero group in New York.

From New York and Chicago the movement began to spread as the immigrants increased in number. At first, it was concentrated mainly in the large port cities on the eastern seaboard, where the immigrants tended to settle when they arrived. Consequently, by the early 1890s we find Italian anarchist groups in such places as Boston and Philadelphia besides New York. From the east, the movement gradually filtered westward, with small groups appearing in Pittsburgh, Cleveland, and Detroit. Finally, by the mid-1890s we have groups as far west as the Pacific coast, the first Italian anarchist group in San Francisco being founded in 1894.

Among the events which gave an impetus to the formation of these groups was the Haymarket Affair of 1886 and 1887. It is often said in history books that the explosion in Chicago's Haymarket Square on May 4, 1886, which caused the death of seven policemen and led to the hanging of four anarchists and the suicide of a fifth in his cell, precipitated the downfall of the anarchist movement in the United States, because the authorities proceeded to crush the movement in Chicago and to suppress it in New York and other cities around the country. Precisely the opposite was the case. The Haymarket executions stimulated the growth of the anarchist movement both among native Americans and immigrants, and there was a rapid rise in the number of Italian anarchist groups after 1887. November 11, 1887, marks a key date in the history of anarchism in the United States and around the world. That was the date of the hanging of the four anarchists, who were demonstrably innocent of any connection with the bomb-throwing. The fact that these men were ready to sacrifice their lives for their fellow workers was so moving to many young people around the country, some of them newly arrived, that they began to read anarchist literature and to join anarchist groups.

A second important event was the arrival from Italy of a series of distinguished anarchist writers and speakers. Beginning in the 1890s, virtually every famous Italian anarchist visited our shores. Some stayed only three or four weeks, some several years, and a few, like Luigi Galleani and Carlo Tresca, remained for much longer periods of time. I'd like to tell you a little bit about them and about their impact on the anarchist movement.

The first major figure to arrive here was Francesco Saverio Merlino, who came to New York City in 1892, at a very early phase of the movement. Merlino had not only a beautiful command of his native Italian, but he also spoke English quite fluently, having lived in London for a number of years before coming to the United States. This, by the way, was not always the case with the leading Italian anarchists in America, to say nothing of the rank and file, whose English often left much to be desired. But Merlino had this great advantage. As a result, he was not only able to found one of the earliest Italian anarchist journals in this country, *Il Grido degli Oppressi* (The Cry of the Oppressed), but he also founded an English-language anarchist journal called *Solidarity*, which appealed to native Americans as well as to Italians who were beginning to learn the language of their adopted land. In addition to founding these papers, Merlino conducted a speaking tour through the United States, remaining for some months in Chicago. His propaganda, both oral and written, gave anarchism another strong impetus, and so it was unfortunate for the movement that he should have returned to London in 1893.

But Merlino was only the first of a whole series of anarchist spokesmen. The second, Pietro Gori, who arrived in New York in 1895, had an even greater impact on the growth of the movement. Gori spent a whole year in the United States. Like Merlino, he was trained in the law, as was Luigi Galleani. (The rank and file, as I have noted, were virtually all working people.) These leaders, coming from middle-class and upper middle-class families, were akin to the Russian Populists, those conscience-stricken noblemen, Bakunin and Kropotkin among them, who felt that they had a debt to the people and went to teach the people about revolution. Gori too was from a prosperous family, a university graduate, a lawyer by profession, who cast his lot among the working people. He was a magnetic speaker, a poet and playwright, whose poems were often recited and plays often performed at Italian anarchist gatherings in North and South America as well as Europe.

During his stay in the United States Gori held between 200 and 400 meetings — estimates vary — in the space of a single year. This meant that he held a meeting almost every day. He would bring along his mandolin and begin to sing songs, and this would attract a crowd who would stay to listen to what he had to say about anarchism. In this way he won numerous converts and started many new anarchist groups. He resembled a religious evangelist, a wandering minstrel, going from town to town between Boston and San Francisco, preaching the gospel of anarchism, which to some became a kind of secular religion. Gori, unfortunately for the movement, fell ill after his return to Europe, and died in 1911, at the age of 45, depriving anarchism of one of its most capable and beloved apostles.

I must proceed more quickly now, because I could go on and on about each of these fascinating figures. One of the most impressive, yet least well known, of these speakers and writers was Giuseppe Ciancabilla, who had been born in Rome. (Gori, incidentally, hailed from Messina, Merlino from Naples, Galleani from the Piedmont, and Tresca from the Abruzzi, and the rank and file similarly came from all parts of Italy.) Ciancabilla arrived in America in 1898 and settled in Paterson, New Jersey, a major stronghold of Italian anarchism in the east. He became the editor of *La Questione Sociale* (The Social Question), a paper which

Gori had helped to establish in 1895 and which was now one of the leading organs of Italian anarchism in the United States. Ciancabilla eventually moved westward, settling among the Italian miners of Spring Valley, Illinois. After the assassination of President McKinley in 1901, the anarchist groups were raided by the police, and Ciancabilla was driven from pillar to post, arrested, manhandled, and evicted. All this happened long before the Sacco-Vanzetti affair, but already the Italian anarchists were victims of police persecution. Driven out of Spring Valley, driven in turn out of Chicago, Ciancabilla wound up in San Francisco, where Pietro Gori had lectured in 1895. He was editing a journal there called *La Protesta Umana* when he suddenly took ill and died in 1904 at the age of 32, one of the most intelligent and capable of the Italian anarchists in America. More needs to be said about Ciancabilla, and I would hope that some graduate student in the audience will take up this subject and produce a study of the man and his influence in the movement.

Two of the most celebrated of the Italian anarchist leaders — and I put the word "leaders" in quotes, because the anarchists recognized no leaders in their movement but only guides and spokesmen — were Errico Malatesta and Luigi Galleani. (A third was Carlo Tresca, about whom Professor Pernicone will tell you this afternoon.) Malatesta, also from a middle-class family, arrived here in 1899. But, again unfortunately for the movement, he remained only a few months. He too took up the editorship of *La Questione Sociale*, addressed numerous audiences throughout the east, and helped increase the size of the movement. During one of his lectures, in West Hoboken, New Jersey, the representative of a rival faction, or an individual with some private grudge — the motives of this man, Domenico Pazzaglia by name, remain unclear — pulled out a pistol and shot Malatesta in the leg. Malatesta was not severely wounded, and he refused to press charges against his assailant. I might add that the man who subdued Pazzaglia and took away his gun was none other than Gaetano Bresci, the anarchist from Paterson who went to Italy in 1900 to assassinate King Umberto at Monza, and another figure who deserves further study. On leaving America, Malatesta stopped briefly in Cuba before returning to London. A few years later, he went back to his native country, only to be placed under house arrest by Mussolini — but that is another story.

Finally, we come to Luigi Galleani, who was without doubt the most important figure in the Italian anarchist movement in America, winning more converts and inspiring greater devotion than any other single individual. Galleani, as I have said, was born in the extreme north of Italy, near Torino, and, like Merlino and Gori, was trained as a lawyer, although he never practiced law, having transferred his talents and energies to the anarchist cause. Soon after arriving in America, Galleani became involved in a strike at Paterson, not the great strike of 1913 but an earlier one of 1902, in which he made eloquent and fiery speeches to the workers. Arrested for inciting to riot, he managed to escape to Canada, and then, under an assumed name, took refuge for several years in Barre, Vermont, another Italian anarchist stronghold.

The Barre anarchist group, one of the earliest in New England, had been established in 1894. Here we have a case where anarchists in Italy, the Carrara stone and marble cutters, virtually transplanted their movement in the United States, pursuing their same occupations and beliefs as in the old country. It was among these dedicated men and women that Galleani launched his celebrated *Cronaca Sovversiva* (Subversive Chronicle), one of the best anarchist journals in any language. Galleani edited his magazine on a weekly basis, moving it from Barre to Lynn, Massachusetts, where it continued to appear from 1912 until its suppression by the United States government in 1918.

Galleani was an uncompromising internationalist, who opposed the First World War with all the strength and eloquence at his command. He was, by the way, a great speaker in addition to being a first-rate editor. I would say that he ranks among the half-dozen leading orators of the anarchist movement, along with Johann Most, Emma Goldman, and Sébastien Faure. A moving speaker, he had a lilting voice with a tremolo that held his audience captive. He spoke easily, powerfully, spontaneously, and his bearing was of a kind that made his followers revere him as a kind of patriarch of the movement. But after his paper was shut down by the government, he himself was arrested on charges of obstructing the war effort. "Contro la guerra, contro la pace, per la rivoluzione sociale," was his slogan, "Against the war, against the peace, and for the social revolution." He was deported to Italy in 1918. After Mussolini's accession to power, he was banished to a remote island, where he died in 1931 in his 71st year. I might add that it was to the Galleani wing of the movement that both Sacco and Vanzetti belonged, something which Robert D'Atillio will speak about in greater detail.

I have said that nearly all of the Italian anarchists in the United States were working people. It might be useful to tell you a little bit about the kinds of jobs that they had, before moving on to their radical ideas and activities. In New York City they were well represented among the garment and construction workers, and in Paterson among the workers in the great silk factories. We find them among the quarry workers of Barre, the shoemakers of Lynn, the construction and garment workers of Boston, and the cigar workers of Philadelphia. Speaking of cigar workers, there was a whole community of anarchist cigar workers, both Spanish and Italian, in Tampa, Florida, dating back to the 1880s and 1890s. An indication of the type of people they were is that while they were rolling cigars they had a reader sitting on an elevated platform reading anarchist and socialist literature to them, so that their minds would be developed along with their work skills. Going back north, Italian anarchists were very numerous among the miners of southern Pennsylvania and southern Illinois; and in Cleveland, Chicago, and Detroit they were heavily represented in a variety of trades, as they were in San Francisco and Los Angeles.

Ideologically, the Italian anarchists fell into four categories: Anarchist-Communist, Anarcho-Syndicalist, Anarchist-Individualist, and just plain anarchist, without the hyphen. These categories overlapped; there were no hard-and-fast divisions between them. Vanzetti, for example, considered himself an Anarchist-Communist, which meant that he not only rejected the state but also rejected the private ownership of property in favor of communal ownership. The Anarcho-Syndicalists, among whom Carlo Tresca was a powerful influence, placed their faith in the trade-union movement, a movement which the Anarchist-Communists generally shunned because they feared that a *padrone*, a boss, would emerge within the union with special privileges and authority. They detected the kind of "iron law of oligarchy" which a number of European sociologists, notably Robert Michels, were evolving after the turn of the century. The third group were individualist anarchists, who were suspicious of both the communal arrangements of the Anarchist-Communists and the labor organizations of the Anarcho-Syndicalists, and who relied instead on the actions of autonomous individuals. Some of the most interesting, not to say exotic, Italian anarchist periodicals were published by individualists, such as *Nihil* and *Cogito, Ergo Sum* ("I think, therefore I am," with emphasis always on the "I"), both appearing in San Francisco early in the century, and *Eresia* (Heresy) in New York some twenty years later. Their chief prophet was the nineteenth-century German philosopher Max Stirner, whose book *The Ego and His Own* served as their testament.

There was also a fourth group that I think deserves to be mentioned, if only because it is so often neglected. This group consisted of anarchists who refused to attach any prefix or suffix to their name, but who called for anarchism pure and simple. They sometimes called themselves "anarchists without adjectives," not communist anarchists or syndicalist anarchists or individualist anarchists; and the figure whom they most admired was Malatesta, an outstanding personality and thinker who, like Galleani, is crying out for a student to come along and write his biography. (Professor Pernicone, it might be mentioned, is completing a biography of that third great Italian anarchist, Carlo Tresca.) In this very audience, one hopes, someone is already burrowing away in the archives and doing the necessary work.

I have said that many of the Italian anarchists, especially of the Galleani school, tended to shun the trade unions. Because of this, the Italian anarchists did not play a conspicuous role in the organized American labor movement, differing in this respect from the Jewish anarchists, who were so prominent in the textile unions, above all the International Ladies' Garment Workers' Union and the Amalgamated Clothing Workers of America. Not that the Italian anarchists were absent from these unions, but their role was not a major one because of their suspicion of formal organizations that might harden into hierarchical and authoritarian shape, with their own officials, bureaucrats, and bosses. The Russian anarchists, by contrast, organized a Union of Russian Workers in the United States and Canada which boasted nearly 10,000 members. Avoiding this type of activity, the Italian anarchists contented themselves with participation in strikes and demonstrations. We have mentioned the Paterson strikes of 1902 and 1913, to which we might add the Lawrence strike of 1912; and we know that Sacco and Vanzetti both took part in strikes in Massachusetts, Sacco at Hopedale and Vanzetti at Plymouth.

In forming groups, publishing newspapers, and agitating and striking for better working conditions, the Italian anarchists were creating a kind of alternative society which differed sharply from the capitalist and statist society that they deplored. They had their own clubs, their own beliefs, their own culture; they were building their own world in the midst of a system which they opposed. Rather than wait for the millennium to arrive, they tried to live the anarchist life on a day-to-day basis within the interstices of American capitalism. They formed little enclaves, little nuclei of freedom, which they hoped would spread and multiply and eventually engulf the entire country and the entire world. After ten or twelve hours in the factory or mine, they would come home, eat supper, then go to their anarchist club and begin to churn out their pamphlets and newspapers on makeshift printing presses. Aldino Felicani is just one example of such an anarchist, and the amount of literature in his possession that Norman diGiovanni described to us last night was only a small fraction, large as it was, of the total output of literature produced by these self-educated workingmen, a token of their dedication and idealism. I would estimate, from my own research, that there were in the neighborhood of 500 anarchist newspapers and journals published in the United States between 1880 and 1940, in a dozen or so different languages. Of these, the number of Italian papers—and this would include the *numeri unici*, the single numbers issued for special occasions—approached 90 or 100 titles, an astonishing figure when you consider that they were produced by ordinary workers in their spare time, mainly on Sunday and in the evening. And in addition to newspapers and journals, a flood of books and pamphlets rolled off the presses, comprising an enormous alternative literature, the literature of anarchism.

Beyond their publishing ventures, the Italian anarchists engaged in a whole range of social activities. Life was hard for these working-class immigrants, but there were many moments of happiness and laughter. They had their orchestras and theater groups, their picnics and outings, their lectures and entertainments. Hardly a week went by that there was not some traditional social activity, but with a new radical twist. Leafing through one of the old newspapers, I recently came across a picnic at the restaurant of Mrs. Bresci, the widow of Gaetano Bresci. Mrs. Bresci was holding a picnic in her restaurant in Cliffside Park, New Jersey. (The police later drove her out of town, and she drifted westward with her two daughters, who may still be alive in California.) Picnics were very important occasions, not merely to dance and drink wine and have fun, all of which was done, but also to collect money for the anarchist press in order to turn out all those pamphlets and journals that I was talking about. New York and New Jersey anarchists made excursions up the Hudson in rented boats, and when they got up to Bear Mountain, or wherever they were going, they would have a picnic, and out would come the food and the mandolins, and then of course the collection.

Lectures were another frequent activity for the Italian anarchists, and especially the lectures of Galleani, whom they prized above all other speakers. The lectures were held in rented halls and in anarchist clubhouses — of the Gruppo Autonomo of East Boston, for example, or of the Gruppo Diritto all'Esistenza of Paterson or the Gruppo Gaetano Bresci of East Harlem, or perhaps of a Circolo di Studi Sociali, a "circle of social studies," hundreds of which existed throughout the country. How do we know about these groups? Look at any anarchist paper, and you will see them listed, with the weekly or monthly contributions of their members, 25 cents, fifty cents, a dollar, and it all added up. In fact, it was these very contributions that kept the Sacco-Vanzetti Defense Committee going though seven years of struggle on behalf of the two victims. That's why there was some point to the voice raised in the front row yesterday. Everybody was talking about Felicani —Felicani did this and Felicani did that, and indeed he did do all those things and was a great, a wonderful man, without whom there would have been no defense effort. But the activity of the rank-and-file anarchists in all those mining towns of Pennsylvania, and all the quarters and half-dollars that they sent in which made up the defense fund, should not be forgotten.

The Italian anarchists also had their dramatical societies, a particularly interesting aspect of the "counter-culture" I have been speaking about. Amateur theater groups in the small towns and large cities put on hundreds of plays, some of them by Pietro Gori, such as *The First of May*. Another play that was frequently performed was called *The Martyrs of Chicago* and dealt with the Haymarket Affair of the 1880s. There was a Pietro Gori Dramatical Society in New York City that lasted until the 1960s and was dissolved only because of the death and old age of its members.

Anarchist schools formed another part of this alternative culture, schools named after the Spanish educator and martyr Francisco Ferrer, who was shot in the trenches of Montjuich Fortress in October 1909. There were Italian and non-Italian Ferrer Schools in the United States, called Modern Schools, a name which suggests what they were aiming for— a school to match the modern, scientific age of the twentieth century, in contrast to the parochial schools, which the anarchists saw as drenched with the spirit of religious dogma and superstition, or the public schools, in which leaders and generals and presidents were glorified. The Modern Schools were schools in which the children were educated in an atmosphere of freedom and spontaneity, in which they would learn about the working-class movement and about revolutions, as well as how to think and live freely. There were at least two Italian anarchist schools that I know about — I'm sure there were more that I don't know about—one of them in Paterson and the other in Philadelphia. Both were Sunday and evening schools attended by adults and children alike.

Finally, a word about celebrations, another example of how traditional modes of life were transmuted into radical occasions and expressions. Instead of celebrating Christmas or Easter or Thanksgiving, the three great holidays for the anarchists were the working-class day on May First, the anniversary of the Paris Commune on March 18th, and the anniversary of the Haymarket executions on November 11th. Every year, in every part of the country, hundreds of meetings were held to commemorate these occasions. In the same connection, one more point might be noted, namely baptisms. One reads of Emma Goldman, for example, making a coast-to-coast lecture in 1899 and stopping in Spring Valley, Illinois, among the Italian and French miners, who bring their babies to her so she can baptize them, not with the names of saints, but with the names of great rebels or of Zola's novel *Germinal*, which was so popular among the radicals of that period.

This, then, is a brief description of the Italian anarchist movement in the United States. I would like, however, to repeat something that I said at the beginning, that Sacco and Vanzetti were merely two rank-and-file members of this extensive movement. They did everything that the others did. They subscribed to the newspapers—one finds in the columns of *La Cronaca Sovversiva* their 25-cent and 50-cent contributions. They attended—religiously, one might almost say — the lectures of Luigi Galleani. They passed out the announcements of these lectures and circulated the literature of their movement, the pamphlets, the leaflets, the journals. They attended the concerts and picnics; one need only read Upton Sinclair's remarkable novel *Boston,* still a valuable source on Sacco and Vanzetti, to see the importance of the "pic-a-nic," as he spells it in his not entirely successful attempt to convert Italian-American English into the printed word. They also acted in the theater groups. Both Sacco and his wife Rosina took part in anarchist plays, as did their friend Vanzetti. They agitated during strikes, something I've already mentioned. They took part in demonstrations. Vanzetti, when he was arrested, had in his pocket an announcement of a protest meeting which he had drafted, and which, I was happy to see, appears in the exhibition of materials on display upstairs from the Felicani Collection. He also, in prison, wrote articles for the anarchist press, some of which appeared in *L'Adunata dei Refrattari,* a successor to *La Cronaca Sovversiva,* which ceased publication as recently as 1971 after fifty years of existence.

To the very end, then, Sacco and Vanzetti remained active anarchists, continuing their work even in prison. Through their articles and letters, through their speeches in court, they were carrying on their agitation, propagating the ideas of their creed. To ignore the anarchist dimension is to ignore the most cherished part of their lives. Let me conclude with a quotation from Malatesta which goes far to explain their tireless endeavors. "The point," Malatesta wrote in *A Conversation Between Two Workers,* "is not whether we accomplish anarchism today, tomorrow, even within ten centuries, but that we walk towards anarchism today, tomorrow, and always."

Nunzio Pernicone:

Thank you very much, Professor Avrich. Our next speaker is David Wieck, Professor of Philosophy at Rensselaer Polytechnic Institute. Professor Wieck will address himself to some of those missing links that I mentioned about Sacco and Vanzetti.

David Wieck, Rensselaer Polytechnic Institute

"What Need Be Said"

Paul Avrich's discussion of the history of the Italian anarchist movement in the United States was not only a beautiful presentation—it is the first statement that I have heard or read that gives a feeling of what that movement was actually like. That movement has been misrepresented, when not ignored, and in histories of the "Sacco-Vanzetti case," where it is very pertinent, it is usually ignored. The picture that has been presented here this morning is one that I know to be true; what I will do, mainly, is to try to add to that picture.

First of all it is important to be clear about the historical context in which that movement developed. Anarchism in the United States was predominantly a movement of immigrant people—the Italians, Jews, Russians, and others of whom Paul Avrich spoke. Immigrants—we do not always remember—were the core of the working class in this country during the latter part of the nineteenth century and the early twentieth century; their exploitation was a prime source of the capital accumulation that built an industrial society and created enormous private wealth for the owners and financiers of industry. It is sometimes thought that the appearance of radical and anarchist ideas among the immigrants could be accounted for by their being aliens—that it could be accounted for by the culture that they brought with them. There is some truth in this but more important for understanding the development of the immigrant movements, I believe, is the fact that in the United States of that time there was something very close to a state of civil war. It was a civil war between the rich and the poor, the people who owned and the people who had nothing or little, between the people who were engaged in establishing the modern capitalist system and the modern American state and people who were opposing and resisting that capitalism and that state. That war was in short a social civil war.

Italian immigrants did, of course, come from a country where traditions of anti-authoritarianism —anti-state, anti-clerical, anti-*padrone*—were strong and the same kind of battles as in the United States were in fact fought out in Italy during the same era. More than immigrants from some other countries, Italian immigrants may have brought with them a certain intolerance toward authoritarian systems. But only a few of them came with radical ideas; they came to seek a better life and found a world that was not very different from the old, and if in Italy they had (most of them) been despised as peasants, here they were despised as Italians. Their life-situations and job-situations in the United States, and the political and economic developments here, were the reasons why many Italian immigrants, like immigrants from other cultures, were responsive to radical ideas, including anarchism. These anarchist ideas the Italian immigrants heard mainly from those intellectuals who escaped persecution at home by going off to the New World, both North and South America, where they helped create new circles of anarchism. Unintentionally, the Italian government contributed to the dissemination of anarchism around the world: the anarchist ideas of the exiles found resonance in the lives the immigrants were living.

To most of us in the late twentieth century, it may seem as if capitalism, and the American state as we know it, existed always. But they were the products of an evolution. Many people in this country—not just immigrants, not just people with radical ideologies and convictions, but also American-born workers, and a great number of farmers — had come to hate the federal government, to hate Wall Street, to hate the banks. The federal government, Wall Street, the banks, represented a capitalism, and a great American state that was becoming a world-power, that they did not want, that they felt was crushing them. Workers fought back and tried to organize unions; as soon as they tried to organize in any industry there was massive, united, and often violent resistance on the part of the employers and on the part of the government. The history of that period, for great numbers of working people, was one of strikes, blacklists, frame-ups, massacres, lynchings, beatings, and the use of the courts and of state militias and federal troops to break strikes. In those hard struggles hundreds of people died. That was the context in which the immigrant anarchist movements developed.

The Italian anarchist movement in the U.S. became known for its justification of violence, and for the background and context of the Sacco-Vanzetti "case" this is of course an important fact. About this I want to say first that for hundreds of thousands, if not millions, of working-people in those years the justification of violence was not really an ethical problem. Many people were against capitalism, many believed in some kind of socialism, sometimes in terms of nationalization of banks or industries, sometimes more vaguely as a simple opposite to capitalism. Such ideas were widespread, and widespread also was the idea that one had to fight back, one had to defend oneself, that there was violence on the part of employers and violence on the part of the state, and that against this violence, workers, farmers, poor people, had to defend themselves. Violence against violence: rifles against rifles: and sometimes dynamite. In the Middle West of my own background, such stories were part of the traditions of the coal miners — the burning of mine-tipples, the dynamiting of bridges of coal-hauling railroads during times of strike, the warfare of Ludlow and in West Virginia. Anarchists were very seldom responsible for these actions — but many anarchists, especially Italian anarchists, openly justified what they thought of as the self-defense of workers and as part of the struggle to achieve a just society.

The anarchists were different from most other people in rebellion against capitalist society and gov-ernment in that they did not believe that by winning union-recognition, or by electing the right government officials, or by building a political party, the problems of the society would be solved. They did not, of course, believe in government. They believed in the need for revolution, they believed that the revolution would necessarily be violent, and many anarchists, especially of the Galleanista movement to which Sacco and Vanzetti belonged, believed in the importance of teaching the necessity of self-defense by violent means and the eventual necessity for popular revolutionary violence, that is, insurrection, the time for which might not be far away.

The reason why it had been easy to convict the Haymarket anarchists, the Chicago anarchists, in 1887 was that they had advocated such a doctrine. (This, of course, was before the time of the Italian-immigrant movement.) Workers had been beaten and killed on picket lines and demonstrations in Chicago and the anarchists had said, "We have the right to defend ourselves." Why? Because the state is not legitimate, the police are not legitimate, they have no right on their side; what they are, is an enemy that stands against the working-people. Anarchists were plain-spoken about what many people practiced and believed but did not so openly advocate.

Some anarchists, particularly those in the Galleani tradition, also justified and believed in the rightness of acts of individual reprisal. Justification of such acts was not always easy to distinguish from advocacy. The great model for such acts of reprisal would be, of course, Gaetano Bresci. Why did he kill the King of Italy? Perhaps I oversimplify — I do not believe that I do — but I think that it was chiefly because the King had honored with decoration the military commander whose troops had slaughtered hundreds of demonstrating farm-workers in the city of Milano just before the end of the nineteenth century. Bresci had left his home in New Jersey and had gone to Italy to kill the King. Anarchists, especially those of the Italian movement, thought that this was a noble action because it was at the same time an act of sacrifice — Bresci gave up his life in order to make a statement about society, about those who ruled the society, about the need and the importance of rebellion by individuals, the overcoming of passivity and submission. He had made a statement that anarchists understood as meaning that people must not wait for leaders to take care of them, not wait for a socialist party to be voted into office and create a new tyranny—a statement that the movement for justice and freedom must come from the resolution of individuals to act in their own behalf. The actions of such men as Bresci were understood as symbolic of that affirmation—and such, I believe, was in fact the spirit of Bresci's act.

Not all of the actions by anarchists, in various countries, that Luigi Galleani recounted in his *Faccia a Faccia col Nemico*—"Face to Face with the Enemy," a book that, I feel sure, played a role in the determination of the Commonwealth of Massachusetts to insist on the guilt of Sacco and Vanzetti, against the weight of evidence—not all of those actions were on the same level of ideal. But those actions were understood as expressing, in one fashion or another, a spirit of individual resistance and rebellion that was essential to the anarchist ideal. Galleani gave intellectual coherence to this ideal—and the Italian anarchist movement in the United States was greatly influenced by that strong figure.

The movement of which Galleani's *Cronaca Sovversiva* was the center was, in a sense, the purest of anarchist movements. By that I mean that its conception of social revolution was one according to which anarchists would not attempt in any way to "run" a revolution or make a revolution. The theory was that it is not anarchists who make revolutions, working-people make revolutions; anarchists educate, anarchists give examples. As Paul Avrich indicated, anarchists give examples in many ways. They give example by the kind of lives they lead, the kind of movement that they build, the kind of social and cultural existence that they have among themselves and with their neighbors, the kind of help (the "mutual aid") that they give to each other and to other working-people and oppressed people. To be anarchist was to rebel, to refuse to be oppressed, not to become an oppressor, to help those who are oppressed. Just that, I would say, is the meaning of all anarchism, not merely of that movement. But I have called the movement around *Cronaca Sovversiva* "the purest of anarchisms" because in many anarchist movements there have been tendencies, of one sort or another, to attempt to lead a revolution; such tendencies the Galleanista anarchists criticized sharply.

The revolutionary anarchists believed that social revolution was possible and not remote. They may have been mistaken but their view was far from irrational. Before 1914 the world—at least the world of Europe and the cultures derived from it, but China also was experiencing revolution—the world was still full of hope. From our perspective those hopes may seem to have been totally unrealistic—but we see that period through the lens of the first World War. When the United States entered that war in 1917, a great wave of repression was mobilized against all radical movements in the United States. The war meant the triumph of American finance-capitalism and of the American state, and it brought down a curtain on the radical movements of the time. As in Europe, that war made an incalculable difference. It gave opportunity for the American government, American corporations, American banks, all working together, to destroy the Socialist Party, the Industrial Workers of the World, the various anarchist movements, all movements that represented any kind of threat, moderate or revolutionary, to the order that was establishing itself. By the time that Sacco and Vanzetti were arrested, the work of repression—misleadingly called "hysteria"—had been done. The Italian-immigrant anarchist movement did not disappear but it gradually ceased to be a significant force, and with the cut-off of immigration its years were numbered.

I don't know if the people who run governments and the people who belong to the significant classes in society bring about wars specifically for the purpose of better controlling society and putting down the rebels and dissidents. I don't know if they do that consciously; sometimes I think so. But war has that effect; and, of course, we live with that same effect in the continuous war, the permanent war-readiness, that is the state of our country. There is always a "threat"—once it was the Spaniards in Cuba, now it is the Russians in Cuba. The appeal is always to national security—an enemy threatens to engulf us.

The deportations of anarchists at the end of the war were one reason why the beliefs and indeed the character of Sacco and Vanzetti were subject to much misrepresentation during "the case" and afterwards. Imagine if Emma Goldman and Alexander Berkman had been in the United States in the 1920's—after three decades in this country they were only technically "foreigners"—imagine what they would have had to say about Sacco and Vanzetti, imagine what a storm they would have sought to arouse. There were no anarchist speakers of that quality in the 1920's. Among the deportees was also Galleani. That most eloquent of speakers and most eloquent of writers — in the Italian language — had been sent back to the land whose prisons and persecutions he had fled twenty years before, where he would experience the prisons and persecution of Fascism.

Sacco and Vanzetti were revolutionary anarchists: without this fact in the forefront, the picture cannot be clear. This was not a fact that liberal sympathizers with the case felt comfortable with. The Communists, who were beginning to achieve a place of power in left-intellectual circles, had their own good reasons not to mention that Sacco and Vanzetti were anarchists — beginning with the fact that the anarchists were the first radical critics of the Bolshevik revolution. Just recently I read a history of American labor from the Communist point of view, and you cannot tell that Sacco and Vanzetti were really anarchists, not from that book. But there has been much falsification of the history of Sacco and Vanzetti, for a variety of political and ideological reasons.

Who, then, were Sacco and Vanzetti? I am sure that we are going to learn a great deal more from the materials in the Felicani collection and I am looking forward to making use of it. Yet there is a great deal already in print that we should simply re-read with more care. Last August 22nd I was asked to speak at a street-rally in New York City, in commemoration of the men, a rally that was held on the steps of the New York Public Library. To the passers-by who paused a bit, some of them to stay, on their way home from work, I tried to tell in a few minutes what Sacco and Vanzetti mean to me. I tried to do that by translating their world into ours. That week, last summer, was, it happened, a week when desperate people in what was being called an "epidemic," were risking liberty and life and the lives of others to rob a few hundred dollars from banks; that day was a day when the news headlined in the tabloids was that in Brooklyn a squad of city-police had emptied their revolvers into the living, dying, and dead body of a small Hispanic man, armed with a pair of scissors, whose mother had (for his sake) called the police; that time was a time when notice was being taken of the "illegal aliens" who are the labor-force of our contemporary big-city sweatshops; and it was one of a sequence of days when what used to be called an Oil Trust was squeezing dollars, gallon by gallon,

from desperate motorists. I mentioned these things and I mentioned other things I had seen in the city that convinced me that Sacco and Vanzetti, alive today, would see a painfully similar world, and would be anarchists. (Instead of a war, that they resisted, a machine of war that never stops running.) That, I said, is part of what Sacco and Vanzetti mean to me. But as to the *persons* — I said that the best thing that anyone in the audience could do, to find out about them, would be to go into the library behind which I was speaking and read three books carefully: *Boston*, certainly; the *Legacy*; but above all the *Letters*. Sometimes, when I read what is written about Sacco and Vanzetti, I wonder if the author has read the *Letters* recently.

But there is something more that I want to say here. What Sacco and Vanzetti signify to me also — to me, as an anarchist — is a force, a strength, of which we should all be capable, a force and strength that we just might encounter among people whom we happen to know. I am phrasing this carefully, because I do not want to call them "ordinary people." That phrase diminishes people; and Sacco and Vanzetti have been too much diminished by those phrases of the Good Shoemaker, etc., phrases that were probably spoken by Vanzetti but, I suspect, with more than a touch of irony. Endless repetition of those phrases adds up to condescension. Good Shoemaker, Poor Fish Peddler, mere *victims*: picked out because, unjustly convicted because, they were Italians who couldn't speak very good English and insisted on talking in court about their weird anarchist ideas, their naive opinions. Innocent of the charges brought against them, they were "guilty" of trying to help bring about a social revolution. That other, perhaps more comfortable, image is a "view," "history," that has to be overcome in order to arrive at a more serious truth about Sacco and Vanzetti.

If I understand Paul Avrich correctly, he was saying that you could have found many people in the Italian-immigrant movement who were doing just the same kinds of things as Sacco and Vanzetti, who would have had many of the same kinds of attitudes, and who would, perhaps, under the same circumstances, have acted very much like those men did when they were imprisoned. How did Sacco and Vanzetti act? This is what matters — it matters more than the fact that Vanzetti was a man of uncommon intellectual abilities. In Sacco and Vanzetti we can see — and if one does not, I do not understand it — we can see persons, individuals, persons of character, persons being true to themselves. These two men were very different individuals, from quite different cultural backgrounds, and their life-experiences were quite dissimilar. Many "sympathizers" did not like Sacco because his way was not as sweet a way as Vanzetti's could sometimes be. They were individuals with identity, very strong identity, and strong feelings. They had not sought a limelight, they had not sought a martyrdom, but in the face of death each man, in his own way, gave example of dignity and courage and loyalty to a faith. In a sense they were great people, great as persons — though not in the sense in which the term "great" is commonly used. The kind of greatness they had is the kind that human beings in general, I want to believe, have capacity for; and in their living, and in their enduring, they exhibited the idea of anarchism, the idea that human beings — why not all of us? — have such capacities.

The marvelous thing that then comes out is — *seven years of an ethical statement*. That statement can be read in the way these men acted, in the kinds of things they said, in what they said in court, in letters, in conversations; but also just in their manifestation of conviction, something one can hear in their "voices," even though one never heard them speak. I don't think that I have to explain this further — it should be the clearest thing in that whole "history," the *Letters* tell it, I think it is enough to point to those seven years.

This, finally, is the importance to me of Sacco and Vanzetti: they were anarchists who exhibited in their lives, in their situation, the meaning of a social and human vision that is for some people just so many words or perhaps a foolish dream. Yes, in a sense they were visionaries. In a sense, but not in the usual and deprecatory sense of "visionary." They were visionary in their lives: their vision was embodied in their lives.

Nunzio Pernicone:

Our next speaker, Mr. Robert D'Attilio, is a refreshing reminder that one does not have to be a college professor or have a Ph.D. to be a genuine historian. In the six or seven years I've known him, I don't think Bob has spent more than 30 conscious seconds of his existence without talking about the Sacco-Vanzetti case. He has devoted his life, I would say, to researching this great tragedy. Indeed, I don't think I would be exaggerating if I said that he is the Sherlock Holmes of the Sacco-Vanzetti case. He has investigated every conceivable aspect of the case, often traveling coast to coast, hunting down old timers, making sure he interviews them before they expire. As a result of these fantastic labors (I say this without intending to give offense to any other authorities who have dealt with the case), Mr. D'Attilio probably knows more about the Sacco-Vanzetti case than everybody else combined. This is especially true with respect to the subject we are emphasizing today: the background of the Sacco-Vanzetti case, the Italian anarchist movement. D'Attilio is the historian who has investigated, analyzed, dissected the anarchist background from every angle, and he will speak to you today about some subject matter that may provide a few surprises. Mr. D'Attilio...

Robert D'Attilio

La Salute è in Voi: the Anarchist Dimension

Before presenting my paper, I want to express my deep regret that a tragic fatal accident has prevented Frank Moloney, the Assistant Director of the Boston Public Library, from participating in this conference. It could not have taken place without his patience, his wise counsel, and his wonderful, civilized sense of the role that Boston Public Library should play in the cultural life of the city he loved. I will miss him very much.

> to try to rescue the
> true face of the Revolution
> from oblivion and legend....
> — Victor Serge

William G. Thompson, the chief counsel for Sacco and Vanzetti during the final three years of their legal struggle, has told us in a very moving memoir that he had been asked by Vanzetti to come to Charlestown Prison just hours before their execution. Vanzetti had come to respect the integrity and the tremendous efforts that Thompson—a Brahmin, a conservative, a lawyer—had made against the legal system he believed in and upheld, to defend two anarchists who had been trying to bring that very system down. Before dying, Vanzetti wanted to thank Thompson for his efforts and to assure him that, though they had not succeeded, they were deeply appreciated. In the course of his remarks Vanzetti strongly reasserted the absolute innocence of Sacco and himself in the Braintree affair, and he also told Thompson that

> ... he now realized more clearly than ever the grounds of suspicion against him and Sacco ...

but that no allowance had been made for his fear as a radical and almost as an outlaw and that in reality he was convicted on evidence which would not have convicted him had he not been an anarchist, so that he was in a very real sense dying for his cause. He said that it was a cause for which he was prepared to die.

Thompson recalled that Sacco had also told him many times that all efforts on their behalf would be useless because no capitalist society could afford to accord an anarchist justice. Thompson had always argued to the contrary, but at this, their last meeting, Sacco — in Thompson's words — "magnanimously did not suggest that the result seemed to justify his view and not mine." Newspapers throughout America reported that Sacco and Vanzetti, faithful to their anarchist ideals, died rejecting any religious rites; they were the first prisoners to do so in the history of Massachusetts. Sacco cried out, "Viva l'anarchia," as they strapped him into the chair. Their actions were a profound shock for most Americans of that day and, for many, additional signs of their guilt.

Therefore, it is hardly an original contention to suggest that the anarchist beliefs and activities of Sacco and Vanzetti, rather than the legal evidence found against them, led to their execution and convinced many of their guilt.

It was a contention, as we have seen, that was made by the two men in the very last moments of their lives.

This is an expanded version of the talk given at the conference.

It was a contention supported by their anarchist comrades and their Defense Committee in the many public meetings they held and in the many thousands of pamphlets they printed concerning the case.

It was a contention that had been irrevocably injected into their trial by their first lawyer, Fred H. Moore—a controversial legal strategy that has been criticized by many, including the later defense lawyers, William G. Thompson and Herbert B. Ehrmann. The issue for the defense was stated quite succinctly by Felix Frankfurter in his book:

> ...the case against Sacco and Vanzetti for murder was part of a collusive effort between the District Attorney and agents of the Department of Justice to rid the country of these Italians because of their Red activities.

It was a contention rejected by Webster Thayer, the trial judge, who asked rhetorically:

> Have Attorney General Sargent of the United States ... and former Attorney General Palmer ...stooped so low and are they so degraded that they were willing by the concealment of evidence to enter into a fraudulent conspiracy with the government of Massachusetts to send the two men to the electric chair, not because they were murderers, but because they were radicals?

Consequently, one might expect that the gathering and examination of facts about the radical activities of Sacco and Vanzetti would have been a chief concern of writers dealing with the case. And, indeed, several of the books written shortly after the execution of Sacco and Vanzetti did make an attempt to deal with such issues, but they did not have sufficient access to necessary information, both official and private, that would have allowed them to deal fully with this subject. (Upton Sinclair's *Boston* is much the best of these, but since it is written in the form of a novel, most readers do not realize that it is also quite accurate as history—more so than most of the other "formal" histories of the case.) Later books, as a glance at their indices will show, dealt less and less adequately, or not at all, with the precise nature of their anarchist beliefs and activities—the anarchist dimension. The most extreme position has been taken by the author of the most recent book on the case:

I cannot agree that the specifics of Italian-American anarchy have much to do with the case. Those who persecuted Sacco and Vanzetti did not care whether they worshipped Galleani or some other prophet; that they were Italian anarchists sufficed.

Justice Crucified, R. Feuerlicht, 1977

The point of this paper will be the opposite of that statement: the specifics of Italian-American anarchism have everything to do with the case; they are one of the most important dimensions of the case; those who persecuted Sacco and Vanzetti did care if they "worshipped" Galleani; the fact that they were just Italian anarchists did not suffice to explain why the powerful forces of the state were mobilized against these two particular men, so relentlessly and unforgivingly, for seven long years.

But, before beginning, let us consider how this situation has come about. How could this dimension, perhaps the most important of the case, be so overlooked despite the floods of words that have been written in the attempt to describe and understand it?

Many crucial government documents concerning the anarchist activities of the two men were sealed and have not been open to scholars of the case until recently.

No author who has attempted a comprehensive historical account of the case has known Italian or used the Italian language sources that contain the information necessary for understanding the anarchist milieu that Sacco and Vanzetti were part of.

The legal aspects of the case have been overemphasized because the majority of the books about the case have been written by lawyers or legal scholars who have quite naturally concentrated their interest upon the trial record and other such legal documents.

And finally, the many dramatic elements of the case—its detective story/whodunnit appeal, the conflict of political outsiders against established society, the sagas of ethnic discrimination and immigration—attracted the attention of many people who knew little or nothing about the anarchist ideas or activities of the two men. As a result much more attention was focused upon the personalities of the two men, leaving the more complex and arcane world of their radicalism in the shadows.

It was the attractive character of Sacco and Vanzetti, the impressive humanity that they expressed so movingly in their words and letters that made much of this attention quite sympathetic, so much so that it caused Vanzetti to marvel, "… they are doing for us what once could have only been done for saints and kings."

Vanzetti's words have an ironical and, in my eyes at least, unfortunate application to the history of the case; for Sacco and Vanzetti, just as countless saints and kings before them, have been turned into myths and legends that have enshrouded the true story of their lives and their ideals. Dramas, poems, novels, paintings, films, all inspired by their struggle for life, have helped to transform Sacco and Vanzetti into symbols, and as often happens in *causes célèbres*, symbols that are rather far from reality.

Perhaps the most remarkable example of such a transformation is the most widely known image associated with the two men: the good shoemaker and the poor fish peddler. The image supposedly comes from the words of Vanzetti, spoken during an interview with the journalist, Phil Stong. These much anthologized words of Vanzetti are:

If it had not been for these thing, I might have live out my life, talking at street corners to scorning men. I might have die, unmarked, unknown, a failure. Now we are not a failure. This is our career and our triumph. Never in our full life can we hope to do such work for tolerance, for joostice, for man's onderstanding of man, as now we do by an accident.

Our words—our lives—our pains—nothing! the taking of our lives—lives of a good shoemaker and a poor fish peddler—all! That last moment belong to us—that agony is our triumph!

Yet the truth of the matter is that Vanzetti never used the phrase "the good shoemaker and the poor fish peddler" to describe himself and Sacco. The source of this image is clearly stated in a letter from Phil Stong to Upton Sinclair (July 16, 1928). Sinclair, while writing his novel based upon the Sacco-Vanzetti case, *Boston*, wanted to use Vanzetti's exact words and had written to Stong for them. In reply Stong said:

…the quotes are pretty accurate I think, and if there is any allowance to be made, it is in Bart's favor. … He did not, of course, say "lives of a good shoemaker and a poor fish peddler." I had to inject that humility and simplicity that was in his presence into my story artificially. That was about the only conscious liberty that I took with his words and I think that it was justified.

Upon reflection one can see that the image seems too self-conscious; Vanzetti would never have mistaken a shoemaker for the shoeworker that Sacco was (he was an edge trimmer), nor would he have described himself as a fish peddler, something that he did for less than a year, and that only during the time he was trying to begin the publication of an anarchist journal, *Cara Compagna*, with his friend Aldino Felicani.

Yet this image, more than any other, has come to symbolize the two men and their struggle throughout the world. Why this is so we can leave to social commentators, but I hope to make the point that such symbols can easily mislead or deceive one about the essence of the case.

Other images of the two men as "philosophical" anarchists, Tolstoyan pacifists, poor and naive immigrant workers, and harmless Utopian dreamers that have been generated by their sympathizers are as incomplete as the images of their adversaries, who present Sacco and Vanzetti as ungrateful foreigners, common criminals, or atheistic anarchists capable of any unspeakable crime. None of these images is comprehensive enough to represent the complexities of the Sacco-Vanzetti case nor the story of their lives.

The time has come to get down to details, to try to show "how things really were" in the lives of Sacco and Vanzetti, to describe their activities as militant anarchists, to understand the anarchist movement that they were part of, and to appreciate the actions of the authorities against this movement. In order to understand the full significance of the Sacco-Vanzetti case, it is time to explore the neglected anarchist dimension.

By militant anarchists I mean people who were actively trying to overthrow the state, people who rejected all religions, and people who, perhaps above all, wanted the freedom to present their beliefs and their ideals openly, to make propaganda for the Idea, as they called their beloved anarchy.

In this paper I will focus mostly upon the connection of Sacco and Vanzetti with the Italian language anarchist paper, *Cronaca Sovversiva* (Chronicle of Subversion), published at that time in Lynn under the editorship of Luigi Galleani, a man whose activities in America have been sketched out for you by Paul Avrich and David Wieck.

Much of the material I will use is unfamiliar, and it may lead to some relentless detail, but I think that such specific detail is needed to show the magnitude and the significance of this overlooked dimension.

Nicola Sacco and Bartolomeo Vanzetti, when they arrived in America within several months of each other in 1908, were neither anarchists nor particularly political. Both came from families that were better off than most of the great mass of Italian immigrants, though they were not by any means wealthy. Vanzetti came from the North, from a family that was deeply Catholic and apolitical; Sacco, from the South, from a nominally Catholic family that reflected the anticlerical strain of Mazzinian republicanism.

By 1913, after five years of living in America, each in his own fashion had become a convinced anarchist, a subscriber to and supporter of *Cronaca Sovversiva*.

The name of Sacco appears for the first time in *Cronaca Sovversiva* on August 6, 1913, on the back page among the short notes and letters which appeared under the heading *Piccola Posta* (Brief Notes). Sacco's note gives an account of money that he and others had raised to help jailed strikers during the recent strike at the Draper factory in nearby Hopedale. It was signed Ferdinando Sacco, his actual name, and the name he always used in his dealings with *Cronaca Sovversiva*; he did not adopt the name Nicola until some time later. During the next few years Sacco's name appears more and more frequently in the pages of *Cronaca Sovversiva*, always in the *Piccola Posta*, attending picnics and conferences, acting in social dramas, continually raising money to aid political prisoners and jailed strikers, always collecting money for "the propaganda." He listened to the many anarchist speakers who came to agitate among those who, like himself, worked in the factories scattered about his hometown of Milford: Carlo Tresca, Elizabeth Gurley Flynn, Joe Ettor, and Arturo Giovannitti, all prominent figures in the famous Lawrence strike of 1912, and, of course, Luigi Galleani. During 1914, by coincidence, the names of Sacco and Vanzetti appear together for the first time in

print, among the list of contributors on the back pages of *Cronaca Sovversiva*; the two men would not meet in person until several years later.

In August 1916 the anarchists of Milford wanted to hold a series of meetings to help the iron workers of the Mesabi Range of Minnesota in their great strike, led in part by Carlo Tresca. They wanted to use the Town Hall, but they were refused permission by the Milford authorities, and the meeting had to be held elsewhere. Later, on December 3 of that year, *Cronaca Sovversiva* reported that the police had arrested three anarchists for holding yet another meeting in support of the Mesabi strikers without a permit; Sacco was among them. He was convicted in Milford and received a sentence of three months, though the charge was later dismissed in Worcester Superior Court.

December was a troubled month for Sacco. Shortly after his arrest his daughter Alba, not yet one month old, died. *Cronaca Sovversiva* in a personal note about her death said, "It was as if she did not value this wretched world of ours, dripping with blood and cowardice."

Despite this personal tragedy, several months later in May 1917, just after the United States had entered World War I, Ferdinando Sacco left his wife and young son to go to Mexico in the company of anarchist comrades. It was now that he met Bartolomeo Vanzetti for the first time.

In the beginning Bartolomeo Vanzetti's search for work and a place to live in America had been wandering and uncertain. His jobs ranged from work as pastry chef in luxurious restaurants to hard outdoor labor. He vacillated between New York and Connecticut, the city and the country, before coming to Massachusetts. It was while working on the construction of a reservoir in Worcester on November 30, 1912, that Vanzetti sent in his 25¢ for his first subscription to *Cronaca Sovversiva*.

Shortly after this, within several months, he had moved to Plymouth, where he found lodging with a fellow anarchist and strong supporter of *Cronaca Sovversiva*, Vicenzo Brini. In Plymouth, like most of the immigrants there, Vanzetti worked for some time at the giant Plymouth Cordage Plant, then the largest such plant in the world, busily prospering as it supplied warring Europe.

In the pages of *Cronaca Sovversiva* the Cordage owners were sarcastically described as hypocritical capitalists, paternalistic Brahmins with a smattering of Ruskin, who tried to keep their workers contented by giving them ping-pong tables for recreation, instead of higher wages. In January 1916 they were unpleasantly surprised by a strike; *Cronaca Sovversiva* militants were in its forefront; and Galleani, much practised in industrial conflict, always ready to fan the sparks of insurrection, came to Plymouth to agitate among the workers.

Though, at the time of the strike, Vanzetti was no longer working at the Cordage, he nevertheless took an active role in it. Not only was he in charge of the money collected to help the strikers, always a trusted and responsible position among the anarchists, but he also sent in reports to *Cronaca* about the progress of the strike, some under his own name, others under a pseudonym, Nespola, a tactic that many anarchists used to avoid the attention of the police.

Bitter disputes between the anarchists and the socialists over strike tactics, in which Vanzetti was often involved, dissipated energies, and, after the strike had lasted one month during a bitter winter, the workers rejected the militancy of the anarchists and accepted the settlement of the owners.

In 1916 the violence in labor conflicts continued to mount throughout America; *Cronaca Sovversiva* militants, Vanzetti among them, continued their activities, agitating, leafleting, raising money for strikers and political victims; Galleani again left the paper for several months to aid in the miners' strike in Old Forge, Pennsylvania, during which he was charged with "incitement to rebellion" and jailed for several weeks before the charges were dropped.

But another volatile element was about to be introduced into America's troubled society. Woodrow Wilson, despite earlier public promises to the contrary, using the issues of military preparedness and "Americanism," kept edging the United States closer to war. He courted the support of "those that are for America, first, last, and all the time." On April 6, 1917, he finally led the United States into World War I.

On May 5, 1917, three years to the day before the arrest of Vanzetti, we come across a curious event; a document now in the possession of his family shows that, for some reason, he took out first papers for American citizenship. Did this show some hesitancy about his convictions? Or is there some other explanation? We do not know. At any rate, by the end of the month, influenced by Galleani's article, "Matricolati!", Vanzetti left Massachusetts to go to Mexico in the company of other anarchist comrades, including Sacco.

I have gone into some detail about the lives of Sacco and Vanzetti so that there would be no doubt about public identification of these two men as militant members of the *Cronaca Sovversiva* group, by themselves, by their communities, and by the authorities.

Now let us consider this trip that Sacco and Vanzetti took to Mexico. It would be introduced into their trial, not only by the prosecution but by their own defense counsel, Fred H. Moore, to explain the lies they had told the police the night they were arrested. The prosecution charged the men lied because they were conscious of being guilty of the South Braintree crimes; the defense tried to meet the charge by claiming that Sacco and Vanzetti had lied because they were afraid of revealing their radical activities, for which they could be deported. The trip was to be a case in point; in the Dedham trial both men testified they had gone to Mexico to avoid the draft; or as Katzmann, the prosecutor, pouncing on the admission, put it in his first words of cross-examination to Vanzetti, "So you left Plymouth, Mr. Vanzetti, in May 1917 to dodge the draft."

Now it was known, and most certainly by the prosecutor, that only U.S. citizens were eligible for the draft; aliens, like Sacco and Vanzetti, were not; they were only required to register. As a result, the testimony that Sacco and Vanzetti gave to explain their Mexican trip is generally taken as an example of their naivete and incomprehension of the America they lived in. For example, Francis Russell, in his book *Tragedy in Dedham*, says

The official notice explained that registration did not mean liability to military service except for citizens or those who had taken out first papers. Sacco and Vanzetti were not liable, but so remote were they from ordinary American life that neither of them understood this.

Tragedy in Dedham, Francis Russell, p. 81

As a matter of fact, this trip is a vivid example of how certain actions which were to be important in the Sacco-Vanzetti trial have been misconstrued by Sacco and Vanzetti scholars and how the trial records and legal documents of the case can be severely deficient in their ability to explain what was really going on.

A little known but authoritative book about the Italian-American anarchist movement, *Un Trentennio di Attivita Anarchica* (1914–1945) [Thirty Years of Anarchist Activities] Cesena, Italy, 1953, compiled by anarchists, some of whom had been comrades of Sacco and Vanzetti, gives the real reason for their trip to Mexico. Under the date, May 26, 1917, it states:

Several score Italian anarchists left the United States for Mexico. Some have suggested [undoubtedly a reference to Katzmann—*translator's note*] they did so because of cowardice. Nothing could be more false. The idea to go to Mexico arose in the minds of several comrades who were alarmed by the idea that, remaining in the United States, they would be forcibly restrained from leaving for Europe, where the revolution that had burst out in Russia that February promised to spread all over the continent.*

Obviously, this was not a reason they could give in a period shortly after the excesses of the "Red Scare," and in a courtroom where the foreman of the jury often saluted the American flag rather ostentatiously before entering the jury box. Instead of admitting the full truth about the Mexican trip—that they had left the U.S. so that they would be free to fight in the social revolution they felt was imminent in Europe — Sacco and Vanzetti chose what seemed to be the lesser danger for them: they said they had gone to Mexico to escape the draft. (Actually this was literally true in Vanzetti's case, since he had taken out first papers and was eligible for the draft; but, for some unexplained reason, this does not seem to have been known to either the defense or the prosecution.)

A vivid indication of the state of mind that existed around *Cronaca Sovversiva* just before Sacco and Vanzetti and their comrades left Mexico (and an example of the cultural dimension of the movement) is provided by a pamphlet published at that time by one of its most active, sustaining groups, Il Gruppo Autonomo di East Boston (The Autonomous Group of East Boston). It is the Italian translation of a play which had great popularity among radical audiences of that time, *La Vigilia* (On the Eve) by Leopold Kampf: it dealt with the lives of Russian revolutionaries on the eve of the 1905 Revolution, who had begun their activities as peaceful propagandists for a better life, before persecution by the government forced them to resort to political and social violence and to sacrifice their lives for the cause. It carried the seeds of prophecy for the Sacco-Vanzetti case.

New rather startling evidence in recently opened federal files shows that the presence of the *Cronaca Sovversiva* anarchists in Mexico was known to the U.S. government. A Department of Justice report written on January 5–6, 1922, while monitoring "Italian Anarchist Activities" in Boston during the Sacco-Vanzetti trial, refers to earlier letters that had fallen into the hands of the Department in 1918. The report contains the partial text of a letter sent from Mexico to *Cronaca Sovversiva* by one Pacco Carlucci, described as an alias — and correctly, I think — of Carlo Valdinoci, a former editor of *Cronaca Sovversiva* who will figure in this account later on. In this letter he talks of some of his comrades who came with him to Mexico. Mentioning Sacco and Vanzetti by name, Carlucci-Valdinoci says that Vanzetti had not yet decided when to return to the United States, while Sacco had already left to visit a brother-in-law in Ohio. (This would seem to date the letter sometime at the end of the summer of 1917, for Sacco had returned to Massachusetts by the end of August 1917.) It shows clearly that the federal authorities had the *Cronaca Sovversiva* group under heavy surveillance in 1918 and that, as a result of their attempts to suppress the group and its newspaper, the names of Sacco and Vanzetti had appeared in their reports.

The attempt to suppress and deport alien radicals by the United States government has been carefully and convincingly documented in William Preston's valuable book, *Aliens and Dissenters*. In it (pp. 184–185) he describes the concerns that the Department of Justice and the Bureau of Immigration had over certain inadequacies—as they saw it—of a 1917 act which they had been using in their drive against radical aliens. They were awaiting passage of new legislation which would remove these inadequacies, but both agencies wanted to act immediately for they felt they were losing their struggle against the radicals. On July 26, 1918, the two agencies held a meeting in which they decided secretly to apply the measures

---

*This and subsequent quotes marked by an asterisk were originally in Italian and have been translated by the author.

in the law before it was enacted. Preston quotes from a memorandum of this meeting in which the new criteria for deportation (which were not to become law until three months later) were set forth; but he is interested only in their use against the IWW. He does not mention that a significant portion of the memorandum, two of its six paragraphs, is directed specifically against another radical group, subscribers to *Cronaca Sovversiva*. These paragraphs state:

3. In the case of Italian anarchists, evidence of their continued subscription to *Cronaca Sovversiva*, the leading anarchist newspaper in the United States, writing articles for publication in this paper, taking subscriptions for it, and transmitting proceeds to the publishers, acting as distributing agents, receiving of bundles of paper sent by the express after it was denied the use of the mails, contributing to or soliciting and remitting money for the Anarchist Defense Fund, and otherwise by their acts, as well as by their words, assisting in the spreading of the anarchist propaganda, shall be considered good grounds for deportation on the charge of advocating and teaching anarchy in the United States.

4. That such of these Italian anarchists as are ordered deported shall be removed from this country to Italy as soon as possible or practicable, but before such removal the matter shall be taken up with the proper Italian authorities.

Now why was all this time and energy being spent by the Department of Justice, the Bureau of Immigration, Military Intelligence of the Army, Naval Intelligence, and the Post Office to spy on and suppress *Cronaca Sovversiva*, a newspaper that was described by Galleani as "a rag of a paper that lives on crusts and bits of bread, with the support and pennies of five thousand beggars"? (Galleani's estimate of *Cronaca*'s circulation is borne out by its subscription list which had also fallen into the hands of the Department of Justice. It has about 3,200 names. Two addresses show that it dates from before May 1917: Ferdinando Sacco, 76 Hayward Street, Milford, and Bartolomeo Vanzetti, Suosso's Lane, Plymouth). While not an insignificant movement, *Cronaca Sovversiva* was clearly not of the size and scope of the

IWW. Why, then, did this band of some five thousand beggars demand so much attention from the authorities?

The answer to this question is *La Salute è in Voi* (Health is within you), a pamphlet published by *Cronaca Sovversiva*. At first, in 1906, it was quietly listed on the back page among the many other titles of the Library of the Social Studies Group. Later it would be more prominently displayed with the terse and somewhat recondite description, "an indispensable pamphlet for those comrades who love self-instruction." *La Salute è in Voi*, at 25¢ the most expensive pamphlet printed by *Cronaca Sovversiva*, was a manual for making bombs and would become the great unmentioned fact of the Sacco-Vanzetti case, unmentioned by the two adversaries who knew of it, the anarchists and the authorities.

The tall, oblong pamphlet of forty-eight pages, written in a very clear, elementary Italian, refers to certain materials in Italian terms, with costs in Italian lire. This makes it likely that it is, or was derived from, the explosives manual written by Ettore Molinari, fervent anarchist, renowned chemist (trained in Switzerland and Germany, later Professor of Chemistry at the Politecnico in Milano), and a friend of Luigi Galleani. The note to the reader and poem at the beginning of the pamphlet were probably written by Galleani. The note states the purpose of *La Salute è in Voi:*

...to eliminate the vulgar objection that subversives who continually preach individual and collective revolt to the oppressed, neglect to give them the means and weapons for it.*

The poem, presumably there to inspire the reader before he encounters the more prosaic demands of instruction in chemistry, says in part:

Thou hast seen
the Passion, the Sorrow, and the horrid slaughter
of undefended right.
Thou hast curst, thou hast wept
harvesting
prison, misery, and affliction.
*　　*　　*　　*
Cursing is sterile; weeping cowardly,
Listen!
History directs you; Science arms you.

From unavenged tombs, killed by disease and
gunshot
your fathers
Entrust you with their vengeance
Be Bold!
Redemption springs from audacious revolt.*

The authorities did not know about *La Salute è in Voi* for some time, but as the social mood in America became more militant and the labor struggle more intense, events would lead them to discover its existence and eventually obtain their own copy.

Let us see how this manual came into the hands of the authorities.

On July 4, 1914, in New York City a bomb explosion in a Lexington Avenue tenement killed three men who were making a bomb, Arthur Caron, Charles Berg, and Carl Hanson. They were all anarchists. This was shortly after the Ludlow (Colorado) massacre, one of the most tragic episodes of social warfare in U.S. history. At a Rockefeller-owned mine, federal troops that were supposedly there to prevent violence suddenly and unexpectedly attacked a tent city that the striking workers were living in with their families. Using machine guns and setting the tents on fire, the troops killed eleven people, mostly women and children. A pitched battle followed in which many score died; only strikers were indicted and convicted; no soldiers were charged. Outrage swept throughout the country; it was especially intense among workers and revolutionary militants. Since Caron, Berg and Hanson had taken part earlier in the demonstrations against John D. Rockefeller at his Tarrytown, New York, home, both police and anarchists assumed that the bomb they had been making was intended for use against Rockefeller.

This event led to the creation of a bomb squad in the New York City Police Department, headed by Inspector Thomas Tunney. The Squad, in the period prior to World War I, would become the largest, most active, and knowledgeable such unit in the United States. Among other groups, it focused particular attention on *Cronaca Sovversiva*.

I should point out, however, that like most bomb squads throughout the world, it hardly caught or convicted anyone. Indeed, its lack of success in solving a series of bomb explosions in New York City led it to use a timeless police tactic, the *agent provocateur*. Two young, impressionable Italians who frequented

the Bresci Circle, an anarchist center on 106th Street, were lured into trying to bomb Saint Patrick's Cathedral and arrested while planting the explosives.

Several days later, on March 13, 1915, Luigi Galleani published a front-page article in *Cronaca Sovversiva* that dealt with this affair (the Abarno-Carbone case as it was called after the two men who were caught), and the recent spate of bombings that had hit New York City; they included explosions in churches on the anniversary of the execution of the Spanish educator, Francisco Ferrer, and an explosion in the Bronx Court House on the anniversary of the execution of the Haymarket anarchists. In this article Galleani charged that the police, unable to face the humiliating failure of their attempts to discover the authors of these deeds, had been reduced to taking advantage of the moral outrage of the young against a corrupt society. But Galleani made it clear to his readers that these other bombings were to be considered

…attentats, more or less serious, more or less successful, and so similar in style that we can deeply admire them. Knowledgeable subversives cannot catalog them among the tricks of the police, though they may be disowned by the 'priests' of organization … like Joe Ettor. They are so alike in style that for once the bestial but dumb police cannot take refuge in the impenetrable mysteries of the Black Hand, and they have to enter into the unexplored world of 'reds' without a church, without commandments, without priests, bounded from the Battery to Harlem by two rivers, impossible to grasp, ineffable, inexorable, like air and like destiny.*

The public sanctioning of such acts was not unusual for Galleani. Earlier, in 1907–1908, he had published a series of ten articles entitled "La Fine dell'Anarchismo?" (The End of Anarchism?) that had been written in response to a former comrade-in-arms, Francesco Saverio Merlino, who had asserted that anarchism was now finished, the dying creed of a diminishing band of militants. These articles (later expanded and printed as a book in 1925) presented his most systematic thinking about the nature of anarchism. In these articles Galleani recast, in his compelling inspirational style, ideas that were current within anarchist circles of that period, Bakunin, Kropotkin, Reclus: the inevitability of the social revolution, the necessary overthrow of the ruling classes by force, the insurrectionary role of the general strike, the unwilled, spontaneous nature of popular uprisings, the dangers of unionism and parliamentarianism, total communism in the economic sphere, etc.; but he was unique among them in his strong emphasis on the efficacy of the propaganda of the deed, the individual act of revolt. He saw it as a necessary intermediary between the Idea (*i.e.,* the ideal concept of anarchism) and the insurrection which would lead to the only justified war, the war of social revolution. Galleani wrote with an almost mystical intensity about such acts:

> ... The Idea is embodied in the martyrdom of its first heralds and sustained by the blood of its believers.
> ... no revolutionary act is conceivable where the rebel does not feel himself surrounded by a certain spirituality of consent and by a broad-based consciousness which is ready to receive him sympathetically.*

He gave a highly ethical, even aesthetic, attitude to such acts of revolt (Bresci's killing of the King of Italy, for example); he saw them as rebuffs to cowardice, submission, and indifference; they redirected history on its road to the final insurrection. Above all, Galleani insisted that any such act could not be repudiated by anarchists, for they had been spurred on by anarchist propaganda.

> It is supreme cowardice to reject acts of rebellion when we, ourselves, have sown the first seed and brought forth the first bud.*

In 1914, Il Gruppo Autonomo di East Boston published the historical counterpart to "La Fine dell'Anarchismo?", a collection of articles also written for *Cronaca Sovversiva*, called *Faccia a Faccia col Nemico* (Face to Face with the Enemy). In this book Galleani, under the pseudonym Mentana, left a record of what he described as militant anarchism in action. His method was to describe the historical and social circumstances that led certain anarchists to commit acts of expropriation and vindication and to contrast his interpretation of events with the official records of their trials, full of the lies and justifications of the state.

During April 1915 Galleani gave a similar account of the Abarno-Carbone trial in New York City in three long detailed articles, each of which was accompanied by a photograph of the *agent provocateur* who had trapped them. In them Galleani warned the readers of *Cronaca Sovversiva* that *La Salute è in Voi* was now in the hands of the police; it had been found in Carbone's room and it had been introduced as evidence into the trial record. This did not at all prevent Il Gruppo Autonomo di East Boston from still listing it among the titles available in its Library of Social Studies, almost right next to the defense fund it had begun for Abarno and Carbone. We can be sure that by this time, 1915, the social remedies of *La Salute è in Voi* were no longer a secret from Sacco and Vanzetti.

In the same Justice Department report that had linked Sacco and Vanzetti to Carlo Valdinoci (let me remind you that this report was written in 1922, during the Sacco-Vanzetti case, but based on materials seized in 1918), the agent speculated that the *Cronaca Sovversiva* anarchists had gone to Mexico to get instruction in the use of explosives. The lessons of *La Salute è in Voi* in the hands of *Cronaca Sovversiva* militants clearly disturbed the authorities.

Matters in Mexico failed to go as the *Cronaca* had intended. The war continued unabated, making their return to Italy impossible, the Russian Revolution did not spread throughout Europe as had been anticipated, and life in Mexico was much more difficult than had been imagined.

Most of the group returned clandestinely to the United States, though several kept to their original intention of returning to Italy for the post-war revolutionary struggle they expected so fervently. Sacco, who had left behind a family, was among the first to return to Massachusetts by the end of summer, 1917. At this time he had an alias, Nicola Mosmacotelli, that he kept until the end of the war, when he would take back his real name of Sacco. He would choose to keep his new first name, Nicola.

Vanzetti returned to the United States, sometime later, stopping mainly at Youngstown, Ohio, for about six months. But he, too, was in Massachusetts by the end of 1918; he, too, upon his arrival in Plymouth gave up the alias he had been using, Bartolomeo Negrini, but he did not grow back the beard he had before he left for Mexico that had earned him the nickname, "Barbetta" (Little Beard).

It is reasonable to infer that both men had taken these measures to avoid the attention of the authorities, for they had returned to America in the midst of a fierce period of repression for *Cronaca Sovversiva*. Several years before the more notorious and widespread "Red" or "Palmer Raids," the massive forces of the United States government were very specifically directed against this journal and its supporters. Time and time again its offices were raided, its issues confiscated and refused the mails, its editors arrested.

As a result of these raids, contrary to later public statements of federal officials, other material identifying Sacco and Vanzetti as more than ordinary subscribers found its way into Department of Justice files.

These files contained a postcard from Ferdinando Sacco addressed to *Cronaca Sovversiva*. Dated August 10, 1916, one week after the Milford meeting for the Mesabi Range strikers, it said, "In whatever concerns *Cronaca Sovversiva* I am with you. Yours for the revolution."

Two letters from Vanzetti addressed to *Cronaca* in September of that year were also listed as having been confiscated, but no mention of their contents was made; there was also mention of a photograph of Vanzetti taken together with Galleani. (This material, though listed in Department of Justice indices is presently not recoverable from their files.) And we must also remember that the Department of Justice knew that Sacco and Vanzetti were in Mexico with Carlo Valdinoci and other anarchist comrades.

By July 18, 1918, the United States government, by its actions—many of them illegal—had stopped *Cronaca Sovversiva* from publishing openly (two clandestine issues would appear in 1919); by the end of the year it had arrested, deported or forced its militants underground; and its files contained information connecting Sacco and Vanzetti with *Cronaca Sovversiva*, Luigi Galleani, and Carlo Valdinoci. The federal authorities had entered the once "unexplored world of the reds" with a vengeance.

But though *Cronaca Sovversiva* had been suppressed, it would not yet disappear from America's attention.

In the week preceding May 1, 1919, more than two dozen packages with explosives in them were mailed to addresses throughout the country. It was only by chance that practically all were intercepted; only one

exploded, injuring two people. These deadly packages had been sent to public officials and private individuals who had been known for their anti-radical views and activities, people such as Attorney General A. Mitchell Palmer, Commissioner General Anthony Camminetti, Postmaster General Albert S. Burleson, and John D. Rockefeller. Most of them had been specifically involved in actions directed against *Cronaca Sovversiva*.

The shock created by these attempted bombings had not yet died down when a second attack was made on June 2, 1919. This time a series of bombs were set off, all at about the same time, in nine different locations, causing much material damage and two deaths. The most sensational explosion occurred in Washington, D.C., at the residence of Attorney General Palmer.

It severely damaged his house and blew to pieces the man who was placing the bomb. Leaflets found among his remains proved to be similar to leaflets found at other locations. The leaflet, entitled "Plain Words," said in part:

> …it is war, class war, and you were the first to wage it under the powerful institutions you call order, in the darkness of your laws, behind the guns of your boneheaded slaves…
>
> Long live the social revolution!
>
> Down with tyranny!
>
> The anarchist fighters

Throughout the country *Cronaca Sovversiva* and Luigi Galleani were named in many front-page stories as possible perpetrators of both attempts. Nonetheless, no attempt was made by officials to stop the deportation of Galleani and eight other anarchists of the *Cronaca Sovversiva* group from the United States on June 24, 1919.

Clues led the Department of Justice to suspect that Carlo Valdinoci, a former editorial associate of Galleani on *Cronaca Sovversiva*, a comrade of Sacco and Vanzetti, who had been with them in Mexico, was the man killed at Palmer's house. Though the authorities were never able to prove this conclusively, Valdinoci was never heard of again, and other evidence makes it a fair assumption that he was the man involved.

The investigation to verify this was taken over by

the new, young and ambitious leader of the newly formed General Intelligence Division of the Department of Justice, J. Edgar Hoover. Hoover's efforts led to the arrest of two printers of the small anarchist journal, *Domani*, Roberto Elia and Andrea Salsedo, both of whom had been close friends of Galleani and collaborators with *Cronaca Sovversiva*. The men, under suspicion of having printed the leaflet, "Plain Words," were arrested at the end of February 1920 and questioned intensely about the May 1 and June 2 bombing attempts.

In the midst of these events a robbery and brutal murder took place on April 15, 1920, at South Braintree, Massachusetts. The criminals escaped.

On April 25 anarchist comrades in the Boston area — Sacco, Vanzetti and his new friend, Aldino Felicani, among them — met at the hall of Il Gruppo Autonomo di East Boston in Maverick Square to rally help for Salsedo and Elia. Not having much information, they sent Vanzetti to New York City to find out what was happening. Vanzetti went to see Carlo Tresca, good friend of Aldino Felicani and editor of the anarchist journal, *Il Martello* (The Hammer). He was in the forefront of the legal battles to aid the victims of the govenment's anti-radical drive. Tresca did not know much, for Elia and Salsedo were being held incommunicado by the Department of Justice. He did, however, urge Vanzetti and the comrades in Massachusetts to get rid of any radical literature and materials that were in their possession; more raids were anticipated, and it was best to be cautious in these dangerous times.

On his return to Boston at their Sunday meeting on May 2 in East Boston, Vanzetti repeated Tresca's warnings to Il Gruppo. It was agreed that three of the men present, Sacco, Vanzetti and Riccardo Orciani, would meet with another of their comrades, Mike Boda, the owner of a car, some time early in the week to round up and dispose of any such dangerous materials. Vanzetti would have probably reminded everyone that there would be a meeting to raise money for Salsedo and Elia next Sunday, May 9, in Brockton; he would be the speaker.

In the early morning hours of May 3, 1920, from the fourteenth floor, where he had been held illegally, without charge, in the custody of Justice Department agents, Andrea Salsedo fell to his death on a Manhattan sidewalk. His anarchist comrades charged he had been thrown to his death by federal agents during brutal third-degree questioning; federal officials claimed he had jumped to his death because he had become depressed after confessing that he had printed the leaflet, "Plain Words." The *Boston Herald* of May 4, 1920, carried a front-page article, "Suicide Bares Bomb Arrests," that stated Elia and Salsedo had been helping the government round up members of that "Galleani group of bombers" which had "staged the death conspiracy of June 1919." No longer were the anarchists of *Cronaca Sovversiva*, as Galleani had once claimed, "impossible to grasp, ineffable, inexorable, like air and like destiny"; now much of America had turned into a deadly hunting ground for them.

Within several days of Salsedo's death, on May 5, 1920, Nicola Sacco and Bartolomeo Vanzetti fell into a police trap for the South Braintree murders that had been set for others. As a result of it, their comrade, Riccardo Orciani, was also arrested on the following day, but, because of an unbreakable alibi, he was released within a week.

The trap had been set, because of suspicions aroused by two other anarchist comrades, Feruccio Coacci and Mike Boda. I will not attempt a narrative of the events that led to the arrest, but it is instructive to look at the others who had fallen under the suspicion of the police.

Feruccio Coacci — At the time of the Braintree and Bridgewater crimes he lived in East Bridgewater. In 1918 he had been arrested by the local authorities there under the direction of the Department of Justice as an alien anarchist, who supported *Cronaca Sovversiva*. He was also known publicly as an anarchist because of the many dramas he staged with his dramatic society, Il Filodrammatica di Quincy, and the small anarchist library that he made available to all interested readers. His name appeared often in *Cronaca Sovversiva*, signed to letters and brief notices.

The local Bridgewater police chief, Michael Stewart, who had arrested Coacci in 1918, by his own admission suspected him of the Braintree crime simply because he was an anarchist capable of such crimes. But since Coacci had been deported on April 19, 1920, four days after the Braintree crime, Stewart transferred his suspicions to Coacci's boarder, Mike Boda.

Mike Boda — The real name of Boda was Mario Buda, but unlike Sacco and Vanzetti, with whom he had been in Mexico, he did not change his alias on his return to Massachusetts. Boda had been identified with *Cronaca Sovversiva* for some ten years. He had been with a group in Roxbury, Il Circolo Educativo Mazziniana di Roxbury, which had opened an anarchist school for children and was a long-standing member of Il Gruppo Autonomo di East Boston. He had been arrested in 1916 during a wild anti-war riot in Boston's North End that made all the Boston papers and identified him as an anarchist. Stewart used Boda's automobile to set the trap for the Braintree crime.

Riccardo Orciani—A friend of Sacco's from Milford. He, too, had been involved in the Hopedale strike, the Mesabi agitation. His name appeared in *Cronaca Sovversiva* both as a subscriber and a donor.

Though the local police had not expected to catch Sacco and Vanzetti and prior to their arrest probably had known nothing of their anarchist activities, yet they would have suspected from the start that Sacco and Vanzetti might be connected with *Cronaca Sovversiva*. The police chief, Michael Stewart, who set the trap and first questioned Sacco and Vanzetti, had been the one who had arrested Feruccio Coacci in the anti-*Cronaca Sovversiva* drive of 1918. Sacco, when arrested, had upon him the penciled draft of the leaflet for the May 9 meeting that Vanzetti was to hold in Brockton; the language alone would have been sufficient to identify them as anarchists.

> Workers, you have fought all the wars. You have worked for all the masters. You have wandered over all the countries. Have you harvested the fruit of your labors, the price of your victories? …To these questions, on this argument, and on this theme, the struggle for existence, Bartolomeo Vanzetti will speak.*

But now there is even more compelling evidence in the new Sacco-Vanzetti archive that has come to the Boston Public Library, the Aldino Felicani collection (perhaps, the most important single archive concerning the case), to indicate that any suspicions of the police would have been confirmed as fact rather quickly. In a search of Vanzetti's room after his arrest, the police found two unopened registered letters of Carlo Tresca, sent from New York City the day after Salsedo's death. In these letters, opened by the police, of course, Tresca told Vanzetti he knew little about Salsedo's death, and, in both, he repeated the advice he had given to Vanzetti in New York City in words

that could have only aroused the police's attention: "struggi la presente; non conservate mai carte." ("destroy this letter; don't ever keep documents.")

Such letters, written by the notorious Carlo Tresca about the Salsedo affair at a time when it was a front-page story in Boston papers would have been sufficient to suggest to any police official that Sacco and Vanzetti required investigation for more than just the crimes of robbery and murder.

And indeed, the questions that Sacco and Vanzetti were asked in their first interrogations did not deal with either the Bridgewater or Braintree crimes; they were asked instead about their beliefs, their friends, and their activities. The prisoners, undoubtedly with the fate of Salsedo on their minds, tried to give the police as little information as possible; sometimes they lied. With these lies the legal machinery that was to execute Sacco and Vanzetti had been set in motion.

Now let us look, in brief, at the activities of J. Edgar Hoover and the Department of Justice during the few months before the arrest of Sacco and Vanzetti to just before the opening of their trial in May 1921.

Hoover, in his investigation of the June 2, 1919, bombings, immediately set about to collect all Department of Justice files concerning *Cronaca Sovversiva*. The end of World War I and the attendant confusion in Washington's bureaucratic reshuffling had caused many of these files to become dispersed or lost, and it had become a source of irritation to Hoover that he could not track down one of the items he most desired, the copy of *La Salute è in Voi* that had been in the Department's hands. During the months of April and May 1920 he sent letter after letter to every person and every agency that had been involved in the surveillance and suppression of *Cronaca Sovversiva*, but nothing availed; Hoover could not find *La Salute è in Voi*.

(The Department of Justice had found its own copy of *La Salute è in Voi* during its raids upon supporters of *Cronaca Sovversiva* in 1918. As far as I can ascertain, Hoover never did find the original copy of the manual, nor, up to the present, has it ever turned up in federal files; only its translation into English, made shortly after its capture, remains in federal files. I should note also that the Boston Public Library now has its own copy of *La Salute è in Voi*—a later edition that was distributed *gratis*—in the Felicani Sacco-Vanzetti collection.)

Strangely enough, Hoover never seems to have contacted Inspector Tunney of the New York City Bomb Squad who had just at this time published a memoir of his activities on the bomb squad. Under the rather sensational title, *Throttled*, it contained Tunney's account of the Abarno-Carbone affair, and, among its illustrations, had a photograph of several pages from the actual manual, *La Salute è in Voi*. The book was published by a Boston firm at the end of 1919 and a copy was in Harvard's Widener Library by January 1920.

Sacco and Vanzetti were not formally indicted for the South Braintree murders until September 11, 1920, more than four months after their arrest.

Several days after the indictment, on September 16, 1920, an event occurred which would direct the attention of J. Edgar Hoover and the Department of Justice to the Sacco-Vanzetti trial. There was a terrible explosion on Wall Street in Manhattan outside the Morgan Bank — thirty-three people were killed. Several newspapers quickly interpreted the explosion as a bombing that was intended as a reprisal by the Galleani "gang" for the prosecution of Sacco and Vanzetti. In fact, the explosion has never been clearly proven to be a bombing; no one was ever arrested for it; no substantial evidence was ever produced publicly by any authorities to indicate why the so-called Galleani "gang" was suspected.

Yet, shortly after the Wall Street incident, the Department of Justice, on the testimony of the prosecutor Katzmann placed an undercover agent in the cell next to Sacco's in the hope of getting information about the matter, and Hoover intensified his search for *La Salute è in Voi*, extending it, among other places, to Lynn and to Italy.

It would be hard to imagine that Massachusetts authorities, and especially those involved in the prosecution and trial of Sacco and Vanzetti, were unaware of this intense search for *La Salute è in Voi* and the suspected connection between the Wall Street explosion and the Sacco-Vanzetti trial.

And, indeed, there is evidence to show that Massachusetts authorities were not only aware of such matters but were afraid that they might be the target of a bombing attack. They took a rather remarkable action. They outfitted the Dedham court room, in which the Sacco-Vanzetti trial was to be held, with bomb shutters and sliding steel doors that could seal off that wing of the courthouse in case of a bomb

attack. A Norfolk County official pointed out to me how the cast-iron shutters were cleverly made to match the usual wooden shutters so that no one would notice them.

The search for truth in the Sacco-Vanzetti trial would be conducted in a far more formidable cage than the simple prisoner's cage that surrounded Sacco and Vanzetti during their trial. It was a cage built for fear of *La Salute è in Voi*.

Let me sum up the points that I have wanted to make:

Cronaca Sovversiva, the Italian-language anarchist journal, edited by Luigi Galleani, preached a very militant form of anarchist-communism that advocated the overthrow of capitalism by violent means;

this journal and its supporters were considered a highly dangerous group of revolutionaries by the authorities, federal, state, and local;

from 1914 until its final clandestine issues in 1919, the political suppression by legal or illegal means of *Cronaca Sovversiva* was the unrelenting goal of the authorities;

during this period the authorities and *Cronaca Sovversiva* were pitted against each other in a bitter social struggle that was just short of open warfare; the government's acts of repression, often illegal — surveillance, raids, arrests, and deportations, the use of *agents provocateurs*, the refusal of the mails, perhaps murder — were met in turn by the anarchists' attempts to incite social revolution by their militancy in strikes, protest meetings, anti-war activities, by sabotage, and retaliatory violence; the 'propaganda of the deed', some of whose practitioners received instruction from *La Salute è in Voi*.

Sacco and Vanzetti were militant supporters of *Cronaca Sovversiva*, and participants in these struggles; and this information was in the files of the authorities long before their arrest.

If these points are acknowledged, and I think they must be, they carry far reaching implications for the Sacco-Vanzetti Case; they indicate that the primary target of the authorities was the anarchist group that Sacco and Vanzetti were part of, not the two men as individuals; they indicate that the authorities tried to use the Sacco-Vanzetti case as an instrument to finish off the remnants of this group that had been centered about *Cronaca Sovversiva*; they indicate that the substance of the politics of Sacco and Vanzetti can no longer be ignored, overlooked, or dismissed, if we are to get at the 'real being' of the case.

Let me end by discussing the impact of *La Salute è in Voi* upon these matters and point out the reconsiderations and new developments that it will provoke.

As I have suggested, the bitter social war that existed between the authorities and *Cronaca Sovversiva* turned into the judicial drama of the Sacco-Vanzetti trial. In the courtroom, however, the open and almost unrestrained violence of the two antagonists toward one another would be muted by the legal machinery that enmeshed them both and by the presence of a tremendous world audience. These restraints would impose a common bond of silence upon the prosecution and the defense; neither side would mention *La Salute è in Voi* in any recorded legal proceeding.

The prosecution could not mention *La Salute è in Voi* if they wanted to keep up the appearance of trying Sacco and Vanzetti solely as common criminals and if they wanted to deny the charge of collusion with federal authorities.

Yet the prosecution cooperated with the Department of Justice secretly in placing a spy next to Sacco's cell in an attempt to get information about the Wall Street explosion; they put bomb shutters on the courtroom windows to protect it in case of an attack; they surrounded Sacco and Vanzetti with the largest and most heavily armed guard that any prisoners in Massachusetts had received up to that time; and they searched courtroom spectators for guns and bombs before allowing them in.

The Department of Justice, during the trial, without publicly acknowledging the size and scope of its role in the case, illegally intercepted the mail of the Sacco-Vanzetti Defense Committee, placed its spies within the same committee, tried hard to get information through the State Department and the Italian Government about the possible complicity of Sacco and Vanzetti in terroristic bombings and wanted badly to locate another copy of *La Salute è in Voi*, without success. Clearly Sacco and Vanzetti were not just two ordinary unknown alien radicals; they belonged to a group that had, in the authorities' eyes, the fearful force of *La Salute è in Voi* behind them.

Such activities make Frankfurter's charge of collusion between state and federal authorities to convict Sacco and Vanzetti all the more compelling. (It should be noted that Frankfurter's activities led to his phone being tapped by the State Police in the month before the execution of the two, perhaps as part of the con-

tinual, but never successful, attempt of the police to get information about bombings from Sacco-Vanzetti supporters, even from a Harvard professor.) They raise again unresolved questions about the exact role of the Justice Department in the case — would the opening of their files have saved the two men? turned public opinion against them? or, at least, given them a new trial? Were Justice Department files crucial to these issues destroyed? If so, by whose order?

And finally did Governor Fuller and his Advisory Committee, the so-called "Lowell Committee" in their review of the case know anything about *La Salute è in Voi*? It should be remembered that Inspector Tunney's book, *Throttled*, with its prominent mention and photographs of *La Salute è in Voi*, was printed in Boston at the end of 1919 and a copy was available in Harvard's Widener Library by January 1920. It seems unlikely that it would not have been brought to the attention of Governor Fuller and the Lowell Committee, but, at this time, there is no conclusive evidence to show that it was. The possible effect of *La Salute è in Voi* upon the deliberations of Governor Fuller and the "Lowell Committee" remains a topic to be investigated.

The defense, on the other hand, though it had introduced the issue of radicalism into the trial, could not mention *La Salute è in Voi* during a time of fierce repression against alien radicals for fear of hopelessly prejudicing the chances of the men before a jury. As a result Sacco and Vanzetti testified in the courtroom that they needed Boda's automobile—which had led to their arrest for moving "radical literature" to a safe hiding place. "Radical literature" may have been an euphemism for *La Salute è in Voi* or explosives made under its guidance, for Fred Moore told Upton Sinclair several months after the execution of the two men, that "Sacco and Vanzetti admitted to him that they were hiding dynamite on the night of their arrest and that was the real reason why they told lies and stuck to them." Did Fred Moore's bitterness for being dismissed from the case color his testimony to Sinclair, or was it true? This explanation certainly would have strengthened the defense's attempt to explain the lies of the two men and their resulting "consciousness of guilt," but it would have created other problems, just as dangerous for Sacco and Vanzetti.

At any rate, it is clear that the connection of Sacco and Vanzetti with *La Salute è in Voi* cannot be overlooked; they both knew about it from the pages of *Cronaca Sovversiva*; they may have been trying to hide copies of it or dynamite made from its formulas on the night of their arrest; and, when they were in prison, they, themselves, used its words in an appeal to their anarchist comrades. They appeared in the first number of the Defense Committee paper, *La Protesta Umana* (The Human Protest) that was printed shortly after the Massachusetts Supreme Court had denied motions for a new trial. (It is part of Felicani's Sacco-Vanzetti collection and can be seen on display as part of the exhibition that accompanies this conference.) The large headline reads, "Our prisoners warn us *La Salute è in Voi* (Health is Within You)." The statement of Sacco and Vanzetti, entitled "The Testament of those about to Die," written by Vanzetti and signed by both, ends with the words, "Remember La Salute è in Voi." It is without question a call for help to their comrades, a call for direct action now that their legal means apparently had been exhausted, a cry of defiance hurled at the authorities, who would have understood its meaning.

La Salute è in Voi means that the historian of the Sacco-Vanzetti case must enter the world of anarchist ideas so that he can deal with the role of violence within the anarchist movement; he must deal with "propaganda of the deed" and "direct action"; he must appreciate the intense and agonizing debates among the anarchists that argued the political and moral impact of such actions; the distinction between common crime and conscious acts of social revolt; he must understand that the politics of Sacco and Vanzetti clearly state that violence is necessary to bring about the social revolution, that a revolutionary should oppose authority by force, that a revolutionary should retaliate against the repressive use of force with force, that docile submission to the forces of the state is cowardly; but, at the same time, he must be careful about applying such general ideas to the concrete historical situations that formed the Sacco-Vanzetti case; and he must not ignore the violence of the authorities that brought the men to such ideas.

In dealing with the violence — and the counter-violence — of the authorities and the anarchists in the Sacco-Vanzetti case, the questions are many and complex, the definite answers are few, clear facts difficult to obtain; it is work which in large part, still remains to be done now more than fifty years after their execution.

La Salute è in Voi, the dark part of the anarchist vision, the unmentioned fact of the Sacco-Vanzetti Trial, the unknown fact in all historical accounts, tells us clearly that the history of the Sacco-Vanzetti case must be substantially rewritten, that it must take the full measure of the anarchist dimension in order to reveal the true nature of the lives that Sacco and Vanzetti gave up for their Idea.

*Sacco-Vanzetti Reconsiderations
1979: A Symposium*

Philip McNiff:

For our celebration of this important collection, the Felicani collection of Sacco-Vanzetti materials, the moderator for this afternoon will be Professor Salomone. Professor Salomone.

Symposium

William Salomone:
Rochester University

Thank you. I'll be very brief. As you see the good work of the conference continues as we go along and this afternoon the format and I'm sure the span and the varieties of viewpoints will be somewhat different from the ones we heard this morning.

The composition of the panel, as you see them before you, was not chosen at random, I can assure you. We have with us, and I hope they will forgive the description, two Americanists, Professor Foner and Professor Shenton; an Italianist, Professor Cetti; an Italianist in America, Professor Cannistraro — and I don't know what to do with Nunzio Pernicone! ... You have heard him this morning. He is here to work ... for his supper!

I've asked all the speakers to be brief for two reasons: one, because at some point after each of them has given us the core of his statement, they might exchange views among themselves for a few moments; and, secondly, in order to give you an opportunity to ask them and, if you wish, to ask the other contributors to the symposium — most of whom are sitting before us — whatever questions you wish.

I have made two reservations which I think have been accepted by all our participants, and one is that in their statements — you will notice we purposely did not put any topics, did not pin them down to any specific topics — they will define what they will be saying, and I think that should prove very helpful. The other reservation is that they speak from their points of view as experts in their fields, and then perhaps that they give us, you in particular, the fullest opportunity to ask specific questions concerning things they may have dealt with on a more general level. Without further ado, we will go to them and I hope they will forgive me if I don't give each of them his or her full credentials which are all easily accessible — and this for the sake of saving time. I will call on them in this particular order: Professor Foner first, and then Professor Shenton. Professor Foner will define his own subject and I will not spoil the element of surprise in what he will focus on. Professor Shenton just told me what his subject is, and I am not going to reveal that either! Professor Cannistraro can take good care of his topic, and enlighten us on it. As for Professor Cetti, I will let her specify the topic and you will judge. As to Nunzio Pernicone, I know him too well to have any doubts as to how finely, with what historical light and ... thunder, he will close the "formal" part of this symposium: Now, I give you ... Professor Foner.

Eric Foner:
City College of City University of New York

What I thought I would do and try to be brief about is to suggest, in light of the discussions that have taken place over the past two days, where we should go from here in studying and understanding better the Sacco-Vanzetti case in its fullest historical context from the point of view, as Professor Salomone said, of an American historian. The context of Italian history I leave to others.

I believe that despite all the literature that has been written on the Sacco-Vanzetti case there still is a need to place that case more fully in the context of of the social history of the United States and particularly of the 1920s. Many historians, I think, view the 1920s as truly the beginning of modern America. There is a phrase, which I think is true, that the 20th century begins after 1919. In the United States and elsewhere in the world, 1919 was the year of the last great labor uprisings of the era of industrialization. It was not the end of radicalism, but it was the end of a particular kind of radicalism, of the violent mass uprisings of workers caught up in the process of the industrial revolution, then in its later stages.

By the 1920s we see a different kind of America emerging from what had come before. It's a period in which industry adopts different strategies to the problem of what is euphemistically called labor control. It's the first decade of mass consumption as a mode of integrating workers fully into the social structure, and we heard this morning about the virtual civil war that had existed between capital and labor before this. And mass consumption, the use of mass advertising, higher wages, etc., all this was part of a new strategy to try to integrate workers more fully into the American mainstream. It's the era of the birth of the mass media and a kind of mass culture which is very familiar to us today but was quite new at that time. It's an era, of course, of an attack on labor unions which I'll talk about in a minute but also the Americanization decade, the end of unrestricted immigration from Europe. In other words, the real conscious attempt to forge an American working class, rather than an immigrant working class, shorn of its radical heritage and integrated through the media, mass culture, and mass consumption into the society. It's an era when we see the rise of larger than life symbols, individual symbols, of the new trends in American society; people like Babe Ruth whose visages become widely known on the radio, in the mass magazines and, of course, in the movies. This is the first decade when the movies really get a mass audience. Babe Ruth, Lindbergh, many others we can think of and, of course, symbols of a different kind: Sacco and Vanzetti.

So I think, as I say, the Sacco-Vanzetti case couldn't have achieved the notoriety that it did earlier because the technology and mass media were there to be used by everybody, not only by those who raised the cry of Americanization and the red scare, but also by the Felicanis and others who wanted to use the media to draw attention to this case and in their own way make symbols larger than life of Sacco and Vanzetti.

We need to re-examine secondly the labor history of this period. Those of you who are students of American History will know, of course, that in the last ten years we have seen the rise of what's called the new labor history, really a rewriting of the history of American labor in many periods. But oddly enough in this rewriting of labor history, the 1920s has generally been ignored. It's pretty much still an unstudied period of labor history. It was a period, as I said, in which unions were on the defensive; there was a decline of one million in the membership of unions in this country. The Sacco-Vanzetti case became a lone rallying cry for the beleaguered labor movement of the 1920s. My friend David Montgomery, one of the eminent labor historians of this country, recently was telling me about his experiences talking to Slavic miners and industrial workers of Western Pennsylvania, not Italian-Americans at all, in which the only demonstrations they remembered from the 1920s had to do with the Sacco-Vanzetti case. This was, as I say, the sole rallying cry for a labor movement very much in retreat in that decade.

The importance of the labor movement in the defense efforts has been alluded to by some speakers and I think will become even clearer when the Felicani collection is properly digested by historians. Certainly it's clear from what I've seen of the already available publications of the Defense Committee that until 1927 when intellectuals moved into the limelight it was the labor movement which provided a good deal of the organized support for the efforts of the Defense Committee.

There's also a need, I think — and this may bear further discussion later on this afternoon — to look even more than we have at the role of the Italian-American community in this pivotal decade: the larger issue of the social history of Italy and Italian-America in this period of fascism in Italy and Americanization in this country.

A pamphlet by Dos Passos, "Facing the Chair" (which I notice was exhibited among the materials from the Felicani collection) has as its ironic subtitle "The Story of The Americanization of Two Foreign Born Workmen." Well, what happened to Sacco and Vanzetti was perhaps one form of Americanization; but the wholesale assault upon the cultural heritage of the immigrant communities (and not only Italian-Americans but all immigrant communities in the 1920s), as part of this growing mass culture and its manipulation by industry, is certainly part of the context within which the Sacco-Vanzetti case took place.

We need to look at the lasting impact of the Sacco-Vanzetti case on the Italian-American community. I do not read Italian and I'm not able to study the Italian-American press, unfortunately, but those who are, I think, should write more about this question of what is the impact of this case in the 30s and 40s on the Italian-American community. My sense is — I'm ready to be disproven on this — that it contributed to a kind of closing off of that community in some ways, a driving inward, a movement away from politics. It reinforced a distrust of the larger society which, after all, had been brought anyway by southern Italian immigrants to the United States. After all, it was a saying in the *mezzogiorno*, "the law works against the people." Well, the Sacco/Vanzetti case certainly proved that, if there was any doubt about it, and I think it tended to reinforce a family orientation and a community orientation which could lead to a stronger community but also had strong apolitical and anti-political connotations as well.

We also need to study the impact of fascism and, of course, the struggle against fascism on the Italian-American community in this country. Regarding the two individuals, Sacco and Vanzetti themselves, it was made quite clear this morning, and I fully agree with what was said, that we need to take their anarchism seriously. This does not mean, of course, as the discussion indicated, that we adopt a kind of mental syllogism: anarchists believe in violence; Sacco and Vanzetti were anarchists; therefore they were violent people; therefore they were guilty of this crime. That's not what I'm saying at all. But I think that we do need to take their anarchist ideas seriously which is something that many historians have not done, not only for political reasons as was suggested this morning but because of an unfortunate decline in the study of *intellectual* history as such by American historians. The rise of *social* history in the past ten or fifteen years which has contributed many outstanding studies of the American past has led to an unfortunate denigration of ideas as worth studying in their own right, a kind of reductionism whereby ideas only represent some immediate reflection of the social order. I think we certainly need to move away from that in this area as well as many others in American history.

We need as well, as was emphasized this morning, to move away from the rather sentimental portrait of the good shoemaker and the poor fish peddler which was created by the Defense Committee perhaps for very obvious reasons. It's easier to defend in the press, to generate support for, a good shoemaker and a poor fish peddler than for two committed revolutionary anarchists. But I think there is a danger, a great danger of defanging these two men, taking away their radicalism. I'm reminded of a film I just saw at the New York Film Festival a couple of weeks ago on the Wobblies, the IWW; a fine film in a lot of ways which has, I think, the laudable goal of making a modern audience sympathetic to the IWW. But in doing that it seems to take the tack that the way to make the IWW sympathetic in the present is to make it seem like it's just a bunch of nice liberals, you know, fighting against injustice. They were — whatever one thinks of the IWW — they were not liberals fighting against injustice. They believed in the total overthrow of the system and replacing it with a complete new one. Whether that's good or bad, at least they should be taken seriously on their own terms like Sacco and Vanzetti themselves.

I think the careers of Sacco and Vanzetti as individuals, aside from the case, raise some interesting questions for students of American History which call into question some of our assumptions about the whole immigration experience. Sacco, the good shoemaker. Well, you know, the trouble is when you say the good shoemaker, you think of a cobbler or something. He was a skilled, industrial workman who commanded high wages in a factory, not in a little shoe shop; and by the time of his arrest he had accumulated a significant amount of money in savings. On one level Sacco seems to be a success story in the typical immigrant pageant, coming here impoverished and accumulating a good bit of capital for himself. And yet Sacco, in a letter to his daughter, tells her never to forget "the nightmare of the lower classes, the nightmare of the lower classes very badly saddens your father's soul." What does he mean by the nightmare of the lower classes, especially a person who seems to have succeeded on the terms that America set for itself?

What about Vanzetti, this peripatetic, itinerant man, this man who moved from job to job? He worked all over New England and New York in all sorts of positions until he became this fish peddler. Maybe we should think about him as one of those many thousand — millions maybe — in this period of the so-called tramps, hobos, itinerants, who either would not or could not adjust to the discipline of the new industrial order. He didn't want to go and work in a factory 9 to 5 the way the working class was being shaped at that time.

Vanzetti's experience reminds me of another radical in American history—perhaps this analogy may seem a little odd — John Brown. Certainly from a different background, but Brown (if you look at his career in the 1830s and 40s) moved from job to job, place to place, was a constant failure at a time when most historians see American society as being open to people of talent and ambition and everybody rising in the social order. John Brown just never could quite get it together to make it. He got into all sorts of ventures; every one of them failed. Maybe the experience of Vanzetti and John Brown was more typical than American historians like to admit. Or maybe this is why historians have tended to think John Brown was crazy because he couldn't succeed in the terms America set out for its people.

Well, anyway, I seem to have exceeded my ten minutes so I will close by saying that my point is simply that too often, I think, despite the very good work that has been done on the case, Sacco and Vanzetti are too often abstracted from the total history of this period of the 1920s. They need to be placed back into that historical context. And I certainly believe that this conference is an important step in that direction.

James Shenton:
Columbia University

I would like to continue from where Professor Foner concluded. There are a number of areas where I think significant new research would illuminate further the role of Sacco and Vanzetti in American history. There are three areas which are of particular interest. The first of these is the role of the Roman Catholic Church during the Sacco-Vanzetti case. The second is how did the case affect Italian-Americans? And finally, how was the case used during the debate over the National Origins Act, specifically the closing in 1924 of unrestricted immigration and the establishment of the quota system.

Recently, a friend told me that in his research he found that Cardinal O'Connell of Boston directly intervened with the Governor of Massachusetts to obtain a stay of execution and that this was apparently done at the urging of Vatican authorities. He also noted that Patrick Cardinal Hayes of New York City added his weight to the appeal. When I asked how this effort was coordinated, he said he did not know. It reminded me of a later instance of the Catholic hierarchy's intervention in politics. In 1936, Father Charles Coughlin, the radio-priest, openly attacked the candidacy of Franklin D. Roosevelt. Catholic authorities were deeply concerned by the vitriolic temper of these attacks, particularly when Coughlin denounced Roosevelt as a liar. This concern deepened when pro-Coughlin delegates were elected in a sweeping victory to represent Boston at the 1936 Democratic national convention. Both the Roosevelt and Monsignor John Ryan Papers contain extended discussions on how to counteract Coughlin. An interesting suggestion was that Edward Corsi, a prominent Italian-American from New York City, be used to influence the Vatican, as he had in the Sacco-Vanzetti case.

In the Roosevelt case, Corsi and apparently almost the whole of the Catholic hierarchy used their influence to have Eugenio Cardinal Pacelli, the future Pius XII, attend a Eucharistic conference held in the United States in mid-October of 1936. Pacelli remained in the United States until the day after the presidential election overwhelmingly re-elected Roosevelt. Throughout Pacelli's stay, the hierarchy understood that if Coughlin resumed his vitriolic attacks or if he seemed likely to affect the election result, he, as a spokesman of the Vatican, would publicly disassociate the Church from Coughlin's position. The question that is left is what process governed the Church's posture in the Sacco-Vanzetti case?

A possible approach is one that focuses on the structure of American Catholicism in the 1920's. At its core were the ethnic parishes. The weight of evidence indicates that matters of particular interest to ethnic groups played a major role in the internal affairs of the parish. The predominantly Irish-American hierarchy were acutely aware of the importance of ethnic interests in the parishes. It is unlikely that either O'Connell or Hayes could ignore the impact of the Sacco-Vanzetti case in the Italian-

American parishes under their jurisdiction. In Chicago, the liberal Cardinal Mundelein put pressure on the other Cardinals by openly supporting a pro-Sacco-Vanzetti position and pressing for the Church to take a similar stand. It is worth noting that Mundelein took the lead in mobilizing Church opposition to Coughlin.

Without doubt, given the inter-ethnic pressures that bubbled under the surface of American Catholicism, Sacco-Vanzetti was the issue that Boston church authorities could not ignore. I doubt whether anyone from Boston could be unaware of the acute strains that existed between Irish and Italian Bostonians. Cardinal O'Connell, who apparently worked to mute these strains, may well have felt a positive intervention in the Sacco-Vanzetti case was a necessary concession to Italian-American Catholics in the Boston Archdiocese. A fuller examination of diocesan records and Italian-American parish records would permit a more precise answer.

In the debate over the National Origins Act, especially that recorded in the *Congressional Record* and in publications that supported the Act, there are frequent references to the Sacco-Vanzetti case. More often than not, it was cited as justification for discriminatory quotas. Frequently, the radical and anarchistic reputations of Sacco and Vanzetti were set forth as proof of the country's incapacity to absorb aliens such as Italians. A similar stance was taken by the many business journals. They argued that although the Act would close off sources of cheap labor, the country would benefit from the future exclusion of radicals such as Sacco and Vanzetti.

How exactly Sacco-Vanzetti affected the Massachusetts scene is difficult to determine. J. Joseph Huthmacher, *Massachusetts People and Politics, 1919–1933,* a near definitive account, makes no reference to the case. However, some years ago, while working on the Passaic, New Jersey general strike of 1926, I found an interesting pattern. Time and again in fund raising efforts, the cause of the strikers in probably the most bitter labor confrontation of the 1920's and the cause of Sacco-Vanzetti were often related. Frequently, after the call for striker funds was met, a second call for funds to help Sacco and Vanzetti was made and met. An intriguing sidelight was that Albert Weisbrod, a key strike leader, subsequently observed that this was done to tighten the support of Italian-American strikers.

Since I grew up in the Passaic Valley, a personal anecdote might serve to illuminate further the question of where Italian-Americans generally stood on Sacco-Vanzetti. A significant portion of the Italian-American population in the Passaic Valley were of northern Italian extraction. They came from Veneto, the Piedmont, and Lombardy. It was a population that was important in the anarchistic movement that developed in Paterson and had a strong tradition of cooperative activities. One evidence of this activity was the Italian-American Cooperative Hall, a large public hall, that was frequently used for striker gatherings. In the early part of 1927, a group of Italian-Americans hired the hall to stage a fundraiser for the Sacco-Vanzetti defense fund. When the local parish priest, a Father Agostino of Sacred Heart Church, publicly objected to the meeting, he precipitated a rift in his parish that lasted for twenty-five years. The result of his stand was that he was never able to persuade his parish to fund the construction of a parochial school. Whenever he attempted to raise money for the support of the parochial school building fund, his parishioners responded by dropping two pennies into the collection basket, one for the shoemaker and one for the fisherman. One wonders how an event that gripped a nation for seven years touched an Italian-American population that was most intimately involved?

Luisa Cetti:
University of Milan

I would like to develop very briefly two points that, in my opinion, are worthy of some reconsideration.

The first point concerns the Italian-American community and its internal contradictions in dealing with the Sacco-Vanzetti case. For the majority of the Italian-Americans it seemed evident that Sacco and Vanzetti were persecuted because they were Italians. For this reason the trial produced a certain degree of unity among Italian immigrants of different political views.

Nevertheless, the reactions to the case of the two anarchists provides an opportunity to measure the different opinions and interests inside the community. The most powerful sector of the community, that is the *prominenti,* was overwhelmingly concerned with two aspects of the case: its impact on the future of

Italian immigration, on the one hand, and the political views of Sacco and Vanzetti, on the other.

The imminent restriction of immigration in the early twenties was perceived as a serious threat by the *prominenti* and the Italian government as well. The first Quota Act was passed in 1921 and the second in 1924; both reduced the quota of Italians to be admitted in the United States.

So, neither the *prominenti* nor the Italian government was anxious to provide the American government with new reasons to contemplate even more restrictive legislation. Particularly after the Red Scare, a lot of noise about Italian anarchists could easily have provoked this kind of backlash.

Anna Maria Martellone, an Italian Professor of History, in her book on the Italian community in Boston, gives a clear example of the *prominenti*'s subservience when she quotes the pusillanimous telegram sent by the respectable Sons of Italy of Massachusetts to Governor Fuller, after he refused to pardon Sacco and Vanzetti. The telegram reads:

"We reaffirm our sincere confidence in the integrity and impartiality you have demonstrated towards all the inhabitants of the Commonwealth, and we assure you of our continued friendship and devotion."(1)

It is important to recognize however that the attitude towards emigration was not so homogeneous in the Italian-American community. For instance, Angelo Faggi, an Italian anarchist deported during the Red raids, in an editorial published in the Italian anarchist weekly *Lotta di Classe* (Class Struggle) in 1920 wrote:

"We have to let our workers know all these truths, so that they do not emigrate to the United States where they will find only disappointment, humiliations and persecutions."(2)

Most of the letters and reports from the States published in those years in the Italian anarchist press express the same bitterness. The deported or persecuted Italians who came back to Italy always denounced the image of America presented by newspapers and official agencies in Italy. Instead of there being a demand for labor, they charged that, to use their words, "there is only unemployment, desolation, violence and poverty."

This brings me to the second aspect that divided the community: the political views of Sacco and Vanzetti. The American press in 1919 and 1920 in a very monotonous and repetitive way emphasized bombs, destruction and violence as the characteristics of radicals, in opposition to the so-called "sober common sense and law-abiding character of American people."(3)

By contrast, the Italian-American press developed a bit more original analysis of radicalism. The idea was very simple. People who did not accept American values and American concepts of order must be insane. An article in *Il Carroccio*, an Italian magazine published in New York, entitled "Radicalism and the Foreign Born" in February 1920:

"The foreign born who want to upset American institutions should be treated as paranoics and megalomaniacs."

La Gazzetta del Massachusetts, a newspaper published in Boston, warned its readers against what it defined as "this sort of political maniacs, either bolshevists or IWW."(4)

Thus it is clear that the most integrated and co-opted sector of the Italian-American community could not be very sympathetic to Sacco and Vanzetti. This is particularly true also as regards the Fascist regime. Even when the Italian government's policy toward emigration changed, its attempts to save Sacco and Vanzetti were little more than formal. This is true even if Mussolini in a telegram sent in August 1927 to Sacco's father declared that he tried all he could, consistent with the international law, to save the two anarchists from execution.

I have read all the articles published on the case in 1927 by the most important Italian newspaper, *Il Corriere della Sera*. The tone of these articles is that of hoping for clemency rather than requesting or demanding it. What is more, they underscored their

1. Anna Maria Martellone, *Una Little Italy nell'Atene d'America*, (Napoli, 1973), p. 438.
2. *Lotta di Classe* (Milano), May 1, 1920.

3. *New York Times*, June 4, 1919.
4. *La Gazzetta del Massachusetts*, February 1919, quoted in A.M. Martellone, *Una Little Italy nell'Atene d'America*.

disdain for what they defined "the wickedness of these anti-social agitators" like the two anarchists.(5)

It was Vincenzina Vanzetti, more than anyone else, who gave me a clear idea of the actual behavior of fascism towards Sacco and Vanzetti. She told me how the fascist police came to search her house for letters from her brother, even after he was executed.

If the *prominenti* and the Italian State chose not really to defend Sacco and Vanzetti but to give the appearance of protecting Italian-American immigrants' rights, the American State utilized the fact of immigrant status to discredit the defendants' ideals and all radical-labor dissent.

The second aspect I want to touch is how liberal historiography has dealt with the case.

Sacco and Vanzetti have become after their death symbols: they have become the martyrs of freedom, the victims of a tragic lack of justice.

However, it is necessary to reconsider the Sacco-Vanzetti case in the light of the conditions generated by the Red Scare. The political climate that surrounded the whole trial had its origins in the Red Scare, when intolerance, patriotism, and fear became the prevailing attitudes towards radicalism. In this historical perspective, the arrest, the trial, and the execution of Sacco and Vanzetti appear as the climax of the Red Scare. It was intended as a lesson to all radicals.

Subversion and red peril were, not by chance, cast in the image of the two Italian anarchists. Anarchism, always associated with bombs and violence, evoked fears; and anti-alien feelings were easily aroused when the accused belonged to the most denigrated ethnic group.

If the Sacco-Vanzetti case is viewed in this historical context, it no longer appears only as a tragedy of two martyrs of freedom or as a mere aberration of American justice. It was rather the final outcome of the political choices made during the Red Scare.

The liberal tradition has always considered this period, and consequently the Sacco-Vanzetti case, as a shameful, unworthy, and very sad period of American history, the product of collective hysteria. Robert Murray wrote in *Red Scare* about the Sacco-Vanzetti execution that:

"... the prestige of American justice dropped

so sharply that the damage done to the reputation of American freedom was a long time repairing."(6)

This analysis is limited, however. It does not recognize that the Red Scare was more than a dark page in American history, but the coherent reactions of democratic American institutions toward organized dissent and radicalism, toward the perils of radical changes in the society. Better still, to use the anarchist words, the Red Scare was "the hateful class-vengeance of capitalism."

It is only in this light and considering the whole historical context that the Sacco-Vanzetti case, like the laws against criminal syndicalism and other events in 1920, appear as the weapons chosen to fight the class enemy, organized labor and radicals.

Philip Cannistraro:
Florida State University

I am reminded of Bob D'Attilio's statement earlier today that Sacco and Vanzetti represented different symbols for different people. In this context my work on Italian Fascism and Anti-Fascism may be able to cast a somewhat different perspective on the kinds of things we've been talking about over the last two days.

Looking at Sacco and Vanzetti and the tragedy of their case in the context of anti-Fascism, if nothing else, points out the fact that it was a particular moment, a point of encounter, an example of the crystalization of the anti-Fascist movement in the United States, but also in Europe. If any of you here heard the comments yesterday, particularly yesterday evening, about the Felicani Collection and have seen the exhibit, it will strike you very clearly that there is a direct connection between Italian-American anarchism and the Italian-American anti-Fascist movement. That connection is one which requires a great deal more substantive work before we can reach any final conclusions about it and I certainly have not done that sort of analysis, so my remarks here will be based on some preliminary thinking about the subject.

5. *Il Corriere della Sera* (Milano), August 12, 1927.

6. Robert K. Murray, *Red Scare. A study in National Hysteria, 1919–1920,* (Minneapolis, 1955), p.267.

First of all, what was the meaning of the Sacco-Vanzetti case in the context of the development of an Italian-American anti-Fascist movement? Keep in mind the fact that when the two men were arrested in 1920, there was no such thing as anti-Fascism *as a movement*. It simply did not yet exist; Mussolini had not even come to power, of course. By the time of their execution, in 1927, the major outline of an anti-Fascist movement both here and in Europe existed. Between the time of the arrest and the execution, anti-Fascism matured, grew, it took form, and a number of important events ought to be kept in mind in the context of that growth and maturity: Mussolini's coming to power in 1922, the murder of Giacomo Matteotti, and the consolidation of the Fascist regime in Italy, the suppression at home of anti-Fascism and the exodus in large numbers of Italian anti-Fascists from Italy to countries like France, England and, of course, ultimately to the United States; and, finally the fact that during the years of the Sacco and Vanzetti trial the United States itself was beginning to see for the first time an organized Italian Fascist movement, or at least the presence of one in this country. These are all factors that need to be taken into consideration.

Certainly anti-Fascism had little or no direct bearing on the case itself, but I think it's clear that the Sacco-Vanzetti trial and the tragedy that resulted from it acted as a major symbol. A symbol of what? A symbol, certainly, of the anarchist radical commitment in the struggle to destroy Fascism. Keeping in mind, however, that that struggle against Fascism, whether it be on the part of the two principals, Sacco and Vanzetti, or people like Felicani and Tresca, was a minor point in the wider, broader struggle. Fascism was merely the enemy at that moment. I think this is a point that becomes very clear.

Certainly the Sacco-Vanzetti trial became a symbol for anti-Fascists, not only in the United States but around the world. Just look at the numerous protests in places like Brussels, Paris, London, wherever there were strong concentrations of Italians and particularly anti-Fascist Italians. Look at the kinds of things that Professor Cetti just talked about, *vis-à-vis* Mussolini's attitude. Mussolini kept a very close watch on what was happening in this country. In his demands for clemency he underscored the point that if the Americans executed Sacco and Vanzetti, they would be playing into the hands of the "reds." This was

Mussolini's attitude from the point of view of a Fascist regarding a potential anti-Italian "crisis" in a country where Mussolini and his regime had attracted a great deal of admiration. During the period of the trial and the execution of Sacco and Vanzetti, the first real organized movement of Italian anti-Fascists was formed in Europe, but not until near the end. Consider the fact that some anti-Fascist exiles were beginning to come to the United States for the first time, particularly Salvemini, but not very many were here yet. Also bear in mind the fact that American liberals were only just starting to recognize the dangers of Fascism; a few of them were writing in journals like *The Nation* and so on. But the sense of real danger had not yet permeated all the ranks of American liberals so that what we wind up with is that the major burden of the Italian-American anti-Fascist movement was carried by the radical left, by the labor left. In that context the Sacco-Vanzetti case galvanized many of the potential sources of support that the Italian-American Left would be able to count on later in the struggle against Fascism. It brought many of these forces together for the first time on an issue that wasn't directly concerned with Fascism.

David Wieck's comment struck home this morning, when he spoke of the trauma of Sacco and Vanzetti as seven years of an ethical statement. I think that's very true in terms of this discussion on Fascism and anti-Fascism, because Sacco and Vanzetti represented for the anti-Fascist forces a moral symbol of resistance. And I want to stress the point that it is a resistance against oppression in its generic form, not only in the specific form of Mussolini's Fascism.

If you look at the writings, the letters of Sacco and Vanzetti during the years in prison, you see very clearly a growing awareness of Fascism and of an attempt to come to some analysis of the phenomenon and how to deal with it. From a very superficial analysis of these writings one can come to at least three conclusions: first, particularly in the letters of Vanzetti, there is a very keen, almost prescient analysis of the social, political, the moral forces behind Fascism. When I read of his observations I was struck by the comparisons that one could draw between the observations of the "poor fish peddler and the shoemaker," and some of the analyses of people like Salvemini, Rosselli, and so on — extremely acute observations.

Another conclusion to be derived from their work

is that there was a necessity, as Sacco and Vanzetti saw it, for the creation of a sense of united moral purpose in the struggle against Fascism and that word keeps cropping up over and over again in the letters: we must unify, forget the partisan struggle among anarchists, communists, and socialists — unify for the movement.

Third, and most important, that for these men the anti-Fascist struggle was only a particular moment in a broader, larger struggle that they were fighting as anarchists. And in fact, in many of the letters there are references to the post-Fascist world and the need to continue the larger struggle. Sacco and Vanzetti certainly shared some of the basic perceptions, as I say, of some of the more renowned figures in the anti-Fascist movement like Salvemini and Rosselli. Certainly they would have agreed that the forces that were about to execute them in the United States bore remarkable and frightening resemblance to the forces that had created Fascism in Italy.

Let me just very quickly read you a couple of lines from some of these letters. I think you'll get the point. This one is from Vanzetti to Alice Stone Blackwell on April 14, 1923: "The really and great damage that the fascism has done, or has revealed, is the moral lowness in which we have fallen after the war and the revolutionary over-excitation of the last few years ... the rescue expected and invoked by us must be before all a moral rescue; the re-valuation of the human liberty and dignity. It must be the condamnation of the Fascismo not only as a political and economic fact, but also and over all, as a criminal phenomenun, as the exploitation of a purulent growth which had been going, forming and ripening itself in the sick body of a social organism."

Or this one on September 15, 1924: "The unpolitical masses (in Italy) . . . are dwarfed, brutalized, corrupted, cowardized by thousands of years of slavery, servilism, bestial toiling, sordity, poverty, unspeakable suffering, ignorance, and worst of all, by honors. But, in spite of all the shame, horror and disgrace, they (the masses) are the only ones who look to the stars and not the mud; nor are they guilty. Guilty is the church, the monarchy, the capitalism, the militarism, the Burocrasy, and the yellow, pink, red, scarlet bad shepherds, demagogues and politicians." And then he asked in the same letter, "How will be the future? It will be tears of blood, crimes, degeneration, diseases, insanity and death — or the life and its liberation reached through a terrific lavacrus of blood, through aspiration, heroic sacrifice, and fire. This is the truth. Hard even to look upon." And then at the end of the letter, "The first necessity is to crush fascismo now, and it is a work that requires the cooperation of all the parties contrary to the fascismo." And then finally this letter, again in April, 1923: "This is the great danger, the danger of the tomorrow; the danger, I mean, that, after Fascismo, declined from internal dissolution or by external attack, may have to follow a period of insensate violences, of sterile vendettas, which would exhaust in little episodes of blood (and this is the central point) that energy which should be employed for a radical transformation of the social arrangements such to render impossible the repetition of the present horrors. The Fascisti's methods may be good for those who inspires to *become a tyrant.* They are certainly bad for he who will...collaborate to rise all humanity to a dignity of free and conscient men. We remain as always we were, the partisans of the liberty, of all the liberty."

Nunzio Pernicone:
University of Illinois

After those moving words of Vanzetti's, I don't think I can possibly give you the dazzling conclusion Professor Salomone expects of me. Before proceeding, however, I'd like to make a personal observation. Gaetano Salvemini, whose name has been mentioned several times during the course of the conference, was Professor Salomone's spiritual mentor. In many ways, I look upon the old master in much the same light. In his book *Historian and Scientist,* Salvemini warned about historians who profess complete "objectivity," describing them variously as "happy fanatics" or "wolves in sheep's clothing." Thus, I will make no hypocritical claims regarding my own "objectivity" about the Sacco-Vanzetti case. I am thoroughly biased in their favor. Regardless of whether they were innocent or guilty, railroaded or fairly tried, Sacco and Vanzetti will always command my sympathy and respect. However, while my personal bias will undoubtedly color my thinking about the case, I will always strive to prevent these biases from making me ignore reason or distort truth.

That said, I should like to call the audience's attention to the proclamation issued by Governor Michael S. Dukakis in commemoration of the fiftieth anniversary of the execution of Sacco and Vanzetti. The Dukakis proclamation was not an official pardon; it did not have any legal significance. Dukakis, in the stilted jargon required of his office, said essentially that Sacco and Vanzetti were railroaded because they were ethnics and political subversives — a belief I completely share. A few weeks after the Dukakis proclamation, when *The Nation* (August 20–27, 1977) ran several articles commemorating the anniversary of the execution, Carey McWilliams, the former editor of that magazine and an archetypal liberal supporter of Sacco and Vanzetti, declared that the fighting over the case would finally cease because the enemy had been routed by the Governor's official vindication. In his words, "it now seems unlikely that there will be still another campaign by 'neo-conservative' intellectuals or others, to convict the innocent."

Indeed, in writing the history of this case, one must never lose track of its political dimensions. The attitude of conservatives is best reflected in an article William F. Buckley, Jr. wrote—appropriately enough —in the *American Legion Magazine* of October 1960. He said that the Sacco-Vanzetti case — and I don't think he would retract a comma from this passage today—"was a human vehicle through which to indict the existing order, condemn our institutions, dramatize the cause of proletarian socialism, scrape away at the Puritan ethic, tear and wrench the nation and cause it to bleed across the pages of history." This was Buckley's way of saying that the "myth" of Sacco and Vanzetti (i.e., the "myth" of innocence and persecution) must be dispelled, must be destroyed. The two martyrs of radicalism and labor must be expelled from the pantheon of leftist heroes. Had this not been his purpose, I don't think the *National Review* would have published, within the last seven years, no less than four of Francis Russell's articles on the case, the last of which proclaimed "The End of the Myth" exactly one month after the Dukakis proclamation was released to the press. Clearly, there is a political objective in all this: hammer away at the notion that Sacco and Vanzetti were innocent and their trial a travesty of justice, and thereby demonstrate—as the revisionists have attempted to do for the last twenty years—that the two Italian Anarchists were indeed guilty, and that the Commonwealth of Massachusetts

may be exonerated because it presumably gave them a fair trial.

I'm not going to address myself here to the question of whether or not Sacco and Vanzetti were innocent or guilty, fairly tried or not. I think we've all reached our own conclusions on that score. I would like to say that those of us who take a pro-Sacco-Vanzetti position are obliged to examine every aspect of the case, regardless of how this might jeopardize our own assumptions about their innocence and the conduct of the trial and subsequent proceedings. We must do this because, whether we like it or not, whether we are political partisans or not, anything written about this case, or any attitude manifested toward the key issues, can and will be utilized as political ammunition by people determined to discredit Sacco and Vanzetti. Consequently, it behooves us not only to be as accurate and honest as possible, but to give the opposition its due and hear them out. Unfortunately, Sacco-Vanzetti defenders often have failed to do this. The most recent book on the case, Roberta Feuerlicht's *Justice Crucified*, categorically dismisses every shred of evidence ever produced by the revisionists that suggests that Sacco and Vanzetti might have been something less than 100% pure and innocent. This cannot be. We must get away from the tendency to take umbrage whenever anyone disagrees with us. We must not allow ourselves to be intellectually confined by the emotional passions the case has generated over the years. If there are new aspects of the case that threaten traditional assumptions, that's too bad.

In discussing my own contribution to the literature on Sacco and Vanzetti (see "Carlo Tresca and the Sacco-Vanzetti Case, *The Journal of American History*, December 1979), I will be brief. I am writing a biography of the Italian anarchist, Carlo Tresca, whose statements about Sacco led Francis Russell to change his mind about the case. Russell's first writings (*Antioch Review*, IX, No. 3, Winter 1955–56; *American Heritage*, IX, No. 6, October 1958) asserted that both men were innocent and unfairly tried. Subsequently, in 1962, first in an article for *American Heritage* and then in his book *Tragedy in Dedham*, Russell posited a split-guilt theory: Sacco guilty; Vanzetti innocent. He explained that "the turning point, the way down the mountain for me, was when I learned that Tresca had told Max Eastman flatly, 'Sacco was guilty, but Vanzetti was not.'" This exchange between the Italian anarchist and the noted American Marxist intellectual probably took place around the end of 1942, after whispers reached Eastman concerning the doubts about Sacco's innocence that writer Upton Sinclair had expressed. Sinclair had become doubtful about Sacco many years earlier, while doing research for his novel, *Boston*. Sinclair had been introduced to Rosina Sacco, and simply because she did not fall all over herself being charming and cooperative, he concluded that "there was some dark secret" in the Sacco household. Why it took fifteen years for these whispers to reach Eastman's ears is never explained. Nevertheless, Eastman took it upon himself to ask Carlo Tresca whether there was any substance to the dark rumors Sinclair had circulated. As Eastman explained personally to Russell, there was "one man in America to whom one would go for inside information on what was happening among the Italian anarchists." And that man was supposedly Carlo Tresca. According to Eastman and Russell, who repeats the former's words almost verbatim, Tresca was the "acknowledged and admired leader" of the Italian anarchists in the United States, the man "to whom they turned as a matter of course when they were in trouble," and the person most likely to know their "innermost secrets." Moreover, after Sacco and Vanzetti were arrested, Tresca allegedly "played the part of guardian angel or great-uncle" for the defense. Consequently, "if anyone should have had inside knowledge of the affair, Tresca was the man."

Tresca, referred to only obliquely by Prof. Avrich this morning, was not a movement anarchist. In contrast to someone like Luigi Galleani, Tresca did not create a sub-movement which can be identified ideologically with him. In terms of ideas, Tresca was an eclectic thinker and his anarchism unorthodox. He was, moreover, a true maverick and non-conformist; therefore, it's very hard to put him into any kind of a slot. Tresca was an anarchist, as far as I'm concerned, the most important figure of the Italian-American Left in the 20th Century. Nonetheless, in relation to the theme we emphasized this morning, one cannot make sweeping generalizations about the Italian anarchist movement. The assumptions that people like Eastman and Russell have made, without any real knowledge of the movement, are essentially incorrect. The anarchist movement was not a monolithic bloc, and like all radicals the Italian anarchists were divided among themselves over ideological

questions and other issues. Thus, for reasons which we need not go into here, there was no great love lost between Carlo Tresca and the group to which Sacco and Vanzetti belonged, the Galleanisti. Nevertheless, all the Italian anarchists did turn to Tresca when they needed help because he was the great "fixer," the man who possessed the best connections with lawyers, politicians, etc.; and when an anarchist was in trouble and went to Tresca for help, Tresca would do his best to get him out of it, regardless of his views. But the notion that Tresca was the head of all the anarchists is simply absurd. Aside from the fact that anarchists did not acknowledge leaders, Tresca was the last man to whom the Galleanisti would have said: "you take over where Luigi left off." Furthermore, as we tried to indicate this morning, we cannot be certain that there really were Italian anarchist gangs engaged in expropriationism. Even if we hypothesize that such gangs existed, the anarchists would not have acknowledged the fact; they would not have told everybody in the movement that they were robbing shoe factories. This would have been a very well kept secret. Consequently, it is inconceivable that Carlo Tresca, above all, had to know what was going on, as Russell argues.

My own investigation of this problem has aimed at determining Tresca's real views about Sacco and Vanzetti and evaluating their importance as historical evidence. From interviews and correspondence I have had with his relatives and old comrades, it is clear that during the period of the trial and appeals Tresca believed both men were innocent. He seems, moreover, to have held the same view in the 1930s. But by the early 1940s, between the time of the Nazi-Soviet Pact and the entry of the U.S. into the war, Tresca was overheard on more than one occasion to have made statements similar to those he uttered to Eastman, namely, that Sacco was guilty and Vanzetti innocent.

Apprised of the fact that Tresca's closest associates of the 1920s and 1930s attested to his belief in Sacco's innocence, Russell, in a letter to me, took the position that only someone of absolutely sterling character and with incontrovertible evidence could have been able to make Tresca change his mind. Who was this *deus ex machina*? Russell has no idea. As far as I'm concerned, I doubt that any such person existed. My own suspicion is that the disillusionment and bitterness that resulted from his long fratricidal conflict with the publishers of the anarchist newspaper, *L'Adunata dei Refrattari*, may have caused Tresca to believe that the Galleanisti lied to him about Sacco's innocence from the beginning. This is only a hunch, and I may be completely wrong. What can be said for certain, however, is that Tresca had no private pipeline to Mount Olympus through which he obtained absolute truth about the case. Thus there is no guarantee that anything he said regarding Sacco's alleged guilt is of real importance. Consequently, I would argue that one must not make too much out of tendentious evidence of this sort. If Russell continues to do so, he will only lend further credence to Carey McWilliam's belief that he is a party to the conservative Right's campaign to reconvict Sacco & Vanzetti and expel them from the hall of fame of the radical Left.

Appendix

Appendix A

Chronology of the Sacco-Vanzetti Case
compiled by Robert D'Attilio

1880　The beginning of large-scale immigration by Italians to the United States. Important figures of the anarchist movement F. Saverio Merlino, Pietro Gori, Giuseppe Ciancabilla, Errico Malatesta, Carlo Tresca, Luigi Galleani were among the arrivals.

1886　The Haymarket Affair: a bomb explodes during an outdoor anarchist meeting protesting police brutality in the McCormack Reaper strike. Police fire upon the crowd. Eight policemen and many civilians are killed. The bomb is attributed to anarchists and leads to great public outcry against them.

1887　Four anarchist leaders are executed for the Haymarket Affair; one other commits suicide. There is a great international outcry against execution.

1890　The beginnings of nativist anti-alien, anti-radical movements. Boston is a major center for these movements.

1900　Gaetano Bresci, an Italian immigrant and anarchist, leaves Paterson, N.J., to kill King Umberto I of Italy.

1901　President McKinley is killed by Leon Czolgosz, an avowed anarchist.

Luigi Galleani arrives in U.S.

1903　*Cronaca Sovversiva*, edited by Luigi Galleani, begins publishing in Barre, VT.

The Immigration Act of 1903 is passed as reaction to McKinley assassination. Alien anarchists are barred from U.S. This is the first time in American history that political beliefs are used to bar immigrants to U.S.

1908　Anarchist scare sweeps United States because of alleged anarchist outrages.

Theodore Roosevelt signs federal law directed against the anarchist press.

Ferdinando Sacco and Bartolomeo Vanzetti arrive in the United States.

1912　The great Lawrence Textile strike of 1912. Carlo Tresca is prominent in the post-strike agitation for the jailed strike leaders, Ettor and Giovannitti, falsely accused of murder.

Cronaca Sovversiva moves from Barre, VT., to Lynn, MA.

1913　Draper Co., Hopedale, Mass., strike. Sacco takes part in it and soon after becomes an anarchist and a supporter of *Cronaca Sovversiva*.

Vanzetti becomes supporter of *Cronaca Sovversiva*.

1914　The Ludlow, Colorado massacre: an unprovoked attack by the militia upon striking miners and their families.

Three anarchists, Berg, Hanson, Caron, are killed while making bomb to blow up John D. Rockefeller, owner of the Ludlow mines, in retaliation for Ludlow massacre. As a result, the New York City Bomb Squad is formed.

Aldino Felicani flees Italy because of his anti-war activities and arrives in the United States.

Felicani publishes *La Gioventù Libertaria* in Cleveland and, later, *La Questione Sociale* in New York City.

1915　Anarchists Abarno and Carbone are entrapped by police in plot to blow up Saint Patrick's Cathedral in New York City.

Italy enters World War I.

1916　The Plymouth Cordage Company strike; Vanzetti takes part in it.

The Mesabi Iron Range strike; Carlo Tresca is among the strike leaders.

Sacco is arrested for supporting Mesabi strikers in public meeting.

1917　The United States enters World War I.

J. Edgar Hoover begins to work for Department of Justice.

Sacco and Vanzetti go to Mexico with other anarchist comrades.

The Russian Revolution begins.

Nicola Sacco returns from Mexico.

1918   Under Woodrow Wilson, Immigration Laws are enacted for use against alien radicals.

Cronaca Sovversiva is suppressed and its editors arrested.

Aldino Felicani comes to Boston.

Vanzetti returns to Plymouth.

1919   *May 1:* May Day riots in Boston and throughout country.

Bombs that are addressed to leading figures in the anti-radical drive are intercepted; Attorney General Palmer is among those addressed.

June 2: Bomb explosions throughout U.S. are attributed to anarchists; Attorney General Palmer's house is among those bombed.

June 24: Luigi Galleani and other *Cronaca Sovversiva* supporters are deported.

August 1: J. Edgar Hoover becomes first chief of the Department of Justice anti-radical division and heads investigation of bomb plots.

November 7: First of "Palmer" raids directed against alien radicals.

December 24: Attempted Bridgewater hold-up for which Vanzetti was later convicted.

December: Vanzetti and Aldino Felicani discuss plans for new anarchist journal, *Cara Compagna.*

1920   *January 2:* Second series of "Palmer" raids in 33 cities throughout U.S.

February 25: Anarchist editors, Andrea Salsedo and Roberto Elia, are detained by the Department of Justice for questioning in bomb plots.

April 15: Payroll hold-up and murders in South Braintree, Mass.

April 16–18: Anarchist Feruccio Coacci is arrested in Bridgewater for his activities supporting *Cronaca Sovversiva* and deported from New York City.

April 20: Anarchist Mike Boda, a fellow boarder of Coacci, is interviewed by police, but not arrested. He is suspected of involvement in Braintree affairs; a trap is later set for him at garage where his car was to be repaired.

April 25–29: Vanzetti takes trip to New York City to see Carlo Tresca about Salsedo-Elia affair.

May 2: Meeting in Boston of anarchists; Sacco,

Vanzetti, Orciani, Felicani, and others discuss Vanzetti's N.Y. trip.

May 3: Salsedo falls to his death in New York City while in custody of the Department of Justice.

May 4: Sacco gets passport for himself and family to return to Italy.

May 5: Sacco, Vanzetti, Boda, and Orciani go to Johnson house to get Boda's car.

Sacco and Vanzetti are arrested in trap set for Boda.

May 6: Arrest of Orciani at home.

Interview of Sacco and Vanzetti by Katzmann.

Formation of Sacco-Vanzetti Defense Committee. Aldino Felicani is treasurer.

May 11: Orciani is released.

May 18: Vanzetti's preliminary hearing on Bridgewater charge; he is held for Grand Jury.

May 26: Sacco's preliminary hearing for South Braintree; Sacco held for Grand Jury.

June 11: Vanzetti indicted for Bridgewater hold-up.

June 22–July 1: Vanzetti tried and convicted for Bridgewater hold-up.

August 16: Vanzetti sentenced.

August 19: Fred Moore formally joins Sacco-Vanzetti defense upon recommendations of Carlo Tresca.

September 11: Sacco and Vanzetti indicted for South Braintree crimes.

September 16: Wall Street explosion; it is attributed without proof to Galleani group by newspapers throughout the country.

September 28: Sacco and Vanzetti plead not guilty.

October: Department of Justice begins surveillance of Sacco-Vanzetti Defense Committee; it places an informer next to Sacco in Dedham jail.

Sacco-Vanzetti Defense Committee begins to publish Italian-language journal, *L'Agitazione,* edited by Aldino Felicani.

1921   *May 31–July 14:* Sacco and Vanzetti trial at Dedham. The trial judge is Webster Thayer and the prosecutor is Frederick Katzmann. Both men are found guilty.

October: Mass demonstrations organized by anarchists against the verdict throughout Europe.

1922   *October:* Fascists take power in Italy.

1923   *April 23–September 29:* Sacco is committed to

Bridgewater Hospital for the Criminally Insane.

1924 *May:* Immigration Act establishes quota system and effectively stops large-scale emigration to the U.S. until after World War II.

August: Fred Moore withdraws from defense on Sacco's demand.

October: J. Edgar Hoover becomes chief of the F.B.I.

November: William Thompson takes over defense for both men.

1925 *January–May:* Vanzetti is committed to Bridgewater Mental Hospital.

December: Official Bulletin of the Sacco-Vanzetti Defense Committee begins publishing.

1926 *May 12:* Conviction of Sacco and Vanzetti upheld by Massachusetts Supreme Judicial Court.

May 26: Celestino Madeiros confession of participation in South Braintree crimes is basis for defense appeal for new trial.

October 23: Judge Thayer denies Madeiros motion.

1927 *January 27–28:* Thompson appeals Thayer denial to Massachusetts Supreme Judicial Court.

March: Felix Frankfurter writes article on Sacco-Vanzetti case for *Atlantic Monthly.* Some months later his phone is tapped by Massachusetts State Police because of his Sacco-Vanzetti activities.

April 5: Supreme Court upholds Judge Thayer's denial of Madeiros motion.

April 9: Sacco and Vanzetti sentenced to death by Judge Thayer on July 10.

May 3: Governor Fuller receives clemency petition signed only by Vanzetti.

June 1: Fuller appoints Advisory ("Lowell") Committee.

June 29: Fuller grants 30 day delay of execution to August 10.

July 27: Advisory Committee reports findings to Gov. Fuller.

August 3: Upon recommendations of Advisory Committee, Fuller refuses clemency.

August 7: Demonstrations throughout world.

August 10: Fuller grants stay of execution for 12 days to August 22.

August 15–22: The Department of Justice refuses to open its files to the Sacco-Vanzetti Defense Committee, claiming they contain no evidence of guilt or innocence nor of any collusion between state and federal authorities prior to, during, or subsequent to the arrest and trial of the two men.

August 19: Luigia Vanzetti arrives in U.S. to see brother.

August 22: All legal appeals are denied or ignored. Mrs. Sacco and Miss Vanzetti ask Gov. Fuller for clemency.

August 23: Sacco, Vanzetti and Madeiros are executed.

August 28: Sacco-Vanzetti funeral from North End to Forest Hills Cemetery. The bodies are cremated.

September: All Hollywood newsreels on Sacco and Vanzetti are ordered destroyed by Will Hayes, movie czar.

1927– *The Lantern,* anti-Fascist journal, inspired by
1929 Sacco-Vanzetti agitation, is published by Aldino Felicani and Gardner Jackson.

1937 A bas-relief of Sacco and Vanzetti by noted sculptor Gutzon Borglum is offered to Massachusetts Governor Charles F. Hurley on 10th anniversary of execution August 1937 and it is refused.

1938– Aldino Felicani publishes Italian and English
1951 language anti-Fascist journal, *Controcorrente/ Countercurrent.*

Gaetano Salvemini, Enzo Tagliacozzo, Davide Jona, and many other anti-Fascist refugees are among its contributors.

1947 Borglum plaque is offered to Governor Bradford and Acting Mayor of Boston John B. Hynes, and it is refused.

1957– Aldino Felicani publishes Italian language
1967 anarchist journal *Controcorrente.* Many of its pages are dedicated to the Sacco-Vanzetti case.

1959 *April 2:* Rep. Alexander Cella introduces bill for posthumous pardon for Sacco and Vanzetti to Massachusetts Legislature. The petition is denied.

1967 Aldino Felicani dies.

1974 Department of Justice Sacco-Vanzetti files are opened under Freedom of Information Act.

1977 Fifty years after execution of Sacco and Vanzetti Mass. Governor Michael Dukakis proclaims August 23, 1977, Sacco and Vanzetti day, removing any stigma from their names.

Massachusetts State Police files are opened under Freedom of Information Act, showing Felix Frankfurter's phone was tapped in 1927 because of his Sacco-Vanzetti activities.

Harvard President A. Lawrence Lowell Sacco-Vanzetti papers are opened to the public.

1979   Boston Public Library accepts Felicani Sacco-Vanzetti collection and holds Sacco-Vanzetti conference to mark occasion. Borglum plaque accepted by Boston Public Library as part of the Felicani Sacco-Vanzetti collection.

Appendix B

Program

Friday, October 26, 1979

2:30 p.m.
Conference Opening
Philip J. McNiff, *Director,
Boston Public Library*

SACCO-VANZETTI: THE LEGAL AND SOCIAL ASPECTS

Introductory Remarks
A. William Salomone, *Rochester University*

"Beyond Guilt or Innocence: the Responsibility of History"
Louis Joughin, *historian*

"Brahmins and the Conscience of the Community"
Barbara Miller Solomon, *Harvard University*

"The Idea of Boston: Some Literary Responses to the Sacco-Vanzetti Case"
Daniel Aaron, *Harvard University*

8:00 p.m.
ALDINO FELICANI (1891–1967): MEMORIAL TRIBUTES
On the occasion of the presentation of his Sacco-Vanzetti collection to the Boston Public Library by his sons.

"Aldino Felicani, the Man and His Collection"
Norman di Giovanni

Personal Tributes:
Statements by Oreste Fabrizi, Livio Stecchini,* and Enzo Tagliacozzo.
Anna Yona

Gardner Jackson, Jr.

Description of the funeral procession of Sacco and Vanzetti by Aldino Felicani. Film and Tape.

Introduction
Gabriel Piemonte

Presentation of the Felicani Collection of Sacco-Vanzetti Materials to the Boston Public Library by Anteo and Arthur Felicani

Reception.
Viewing of Sacco-Vanzetti Exhibit.
Boston Room.

Saturday, October 27, 1979

10:00 a.m.
SACCO-VANZETTI: THE ANARCHIST CONNECTION
Nunzio Pernicone, *University of Illinois, moderator*

"Italian Anarchism in America: An Historical Background to the Sacco-Vanzetti Case"
Paul Avrich, *Queens College, City University of New York*

"What Need Be Said"
David Wieck, *Rensselaer Polytechnic Institute*

"La Salute è in Voi: The Making of Two Anarchists"
Robert D'Attilio, *historian*

2:30 p.m.
SACCO-VANZETTI RECONSIDERATIONS 1979: A SYMPOSIUM
A. William Salomone, *moderator*

Panel
Philip Cannistraro, *Florida State University*
Luisa Cetti, *University of Milan*
Eric Foner, *City College of City University of New York*
Nunzio Pernicone, *University of Illinois*
James Shenton, *Columbia University*

*Livio Stecchini died shortly before the conference.

Appendix C

AMERICAN ITALIAN HISTORICAL
ASSOCIATION (AIHA)

Saturday, November 11, 1972
"Italian American Radicalism: Old World Origins and
New World Developments"

Program Chairman
Rudolph J. Vecoli, *University of Minnesota*

9:00 A.M.
REGISTRATION
North Bennet Street Industrial School

9:30 A.M.
GREETINGS
Professor Salvatore J. LaGumina, *President, AIHA*
Mr. Philip J. McNiff, *Director, Boston Public Library*

10:00 A.M.
MORNING SESSION
"Italian Anarchists in America"

"The Italian Anarchist Movement:
The Transatlantic Dimension"
Professor Nunzio Pernicone, *Columbia University*

"The Italian Anarchism and the American Dream—
The View of John Dos Passos"
Professor John D. Baker, *Ashland College, Ashland, Ohio*

Comment
Professor Melvyn Dubofsky, *S.U.N.Y. Binghamton*
Professor A. William Salomone, *University of Rochester*

NOON
LUNCHEON
Various restaurants in the North End

2:00 P.M.
AFTERNOON SESSION
"The Sacco-Vanzetti Case Reconsidered"

"New Approaches to the Sacco-Vanzetti Case"
Dr. Louis Joughin, *Washington, D.C.*

Panel Discussion
Moderator
Mr. Robert D'Attilio

Discussants
Mr. Ben H. Bagdikian
Dr. John Duff
Dr. Nunzio Pernicone
Mr. Francis Russell
Dr. David Wieck

4:00 P.M.
EXHIBIT AND RECEPTION
North End Branch, Boston Public Library

6:00 P.M.
DINNER
Various restaurants in the North End

8:00 P.M.
PRESENTATION OF FILMS CONCERNING THE
SACCO-VANZETTI CASE

Commentator
Mr. Robert D'Attilio

"Nick and Bart: the Ideology of Myths"
Professor David Wieck, *Rensselaer Polytechnic Institute*

21